George Z. F. Bereday

UNIVERSITIES

FOR ALL

Jossey-Bass Publishers
San Francisco · Washington · London · 1973

UNIVERSITIES FOR ALL
International Perspectives on Mass Higher Education
by George Z. F. Bereday

Copyright © 1973 by Jossey-Bass, Inc., Publishers
615 Montgomery Street
San Francisco, California 94111

Published and copyrighted in Great Britain by
Jossey-Bass, Ltd., Publishers
3 Henrietta Street
London WC2E 8LU

Library of Congress Catalogue Card Number LC 72-11624

International Standard Book Number ISBN 0-87589-164-0

Manufactured in the United States of America

JACKET DESIGN BY WILLI BAUM

FIRST EDITION

Code 7308

The Jossey-Bass
Series in Higher Education

PREFACE

Living creatures adopt various forms of social organization. Some live in relative isolation, some in small groups, some in large herds. In order to live in any form of organization, they need to learn; the larger the group, the greater the amount of learning they must have. The more complex the social structure, the more varied the types of learning required. Man, who now lives in vast and complicated societies, must learn how to live with himself, with his family, with his job, with his nation, and with his world. Over the ages, as the clan gave way to the tribe, the tribal village to the city, and the city to the nation, the need for education grew both in size and in depth. First, more and more people had to be brought into the education system in order to prepare them for the roles going beyond mere subsistence which society thrust upon them. Second, the larger the organization, the greater the need for vertical leadership, for people whose knowledge could penetrate "downward" so that, through their acquaintance with the many social activities going on, they might govern or influence the societies over which they presided.

Thus, the edifice of education grew outward and upward. At the outset, mass education might have merely meant nearly universal literacy so that each man could produce more, could have a

voice in the fate of his commonwealth, or could better seek his own
eternal salvation. John Knox wanted all men to have access to the
scripture in the vernacular; Scottish Parish Schools were the answer.
Frederick the Great of Prussia wanted his subjects to be capable
corporals and dutiful taxpayers; hence the *Volksschule* was born.

But not too long after the Volksschule came the Volks-
wagen. A "people's car" is feasible only if the people can drive it.
Technology and education became locked in an upward spiral.
More of one brought demands for more of the other. Yesterday's
ditch-digger became today's power-shovel operator and tomorrow's
electronics technician who may excavate by remote control. To read
the history of the rising tide of primary and then of secondary education in the past two centuries is to understand the condition of
higher education today. The tide of demand surged upward and
upward, submerging the traditional bulwarks of education for the
few. Now the flood is lapping at the gates of the university.

Perhaps by an accident of history, Europe, the mother of
universities throughout the world, was not the first to experience
the crisis. Europeans had spilled over across the seas, carrying with
them their patterns of education, and in one of their new terri-
tories, past the submerged Atlantis, European society and education
found their logical conclusion. In what became the United States,
virtues and vices until then contained by the inhibitions of tradition
flourished freely. Its crusty pioneers insisted that learning formerly
regarded as esoteric was the common heritage of all men, wise or
foolish. As they opened the gates of postsecondary education wider
and wider, the American version of the European university developed. The transplanted *universitas* was transformed into a vast array of institutions catering, each in its own way, to millions of people who never before in history had been thought educable. The
more education was brought within their reach, the more hungry
for it they became. A new lesson began to emerge before the aston-
ished world.

It is no secret that in attempting to reform higher education
the world now tends to look toward these American models. In dealing with any large-scale theme, other countries have been unable to
disregard the achievements of its dynamic and vibrant open system.
Even European countries that gave birth to the university have

come to notice the impact on society of college-educated mechanics and of bookkeepers with diplomas. Other countries leaped ahead to adapt American models to their own needs. To the east of Europe, the Union of the Soviet people, born of a social revolution, has begun building a similar system capable of offering young adults en masse advanced education as well as jobs. Still further east, the gifted Asian people of Japan have superbly blended all the Occidental educational traditions in rebuilding the devastated land of the Rising Sun. This northern geographic circle was recently completed when Canada, with its own mix of American and European traditions, joined the mass-education club.

Time is ripe for a comparative statement about the burgeoning tertiary education of this northern industrial circle. No longer can Europe and the United States be used as the two pivots of comparison in the matter of higher education. More and more insistently, the USSR, Japan, and Canada invite comparison as well. At first glance, their inclusion seems unnecessary because higher education in these three countries retains many similarities to higher education in Europe. For instance, the organization and practices of the teaching staff in Soviet and Japanese institutions appear similar to those prevailing throughout continental Europe. Although differences of definition and measurement make precise enrollment ratios difficult to calculate, the proportion of the relevant age group enrolled in higher education in Japan is no greater than that in France or, for that matter, in the Philippines. In contrast, the proportion of the relevant age group admitted to higher education in the United States is virtually double that of any other country in the world. University traditions of the USSR and Japan and even more of Canada have a historic affinity with Europe. This organizational, statistical, and historical continuum between Soviet, Japanese, Canadian, and European universities would seem to place these countries no more than half way toward the American pattern. Thus, contrasting the United States with the rest of the world seems highly attractive.

This contrast, however, loses much validity if comparative statistics of postcompulsory education are examined rather than conventional statistics which treat higher education as beginning at age eighteen. Taking sixteen as the starting age for postcompulsory schooling, the USSR, Canada, and Japan all retain, like the United States, roughly three-quarters of their youth in at least two more years of education. No European country retains more than half of this age group in study, and most countries do not retain more than one-third. In other words, an enrollment gap of the order of one-fourth to one-third of the sixteen- to eighteen-year age group has developed between these four mass education countries and those of Europe. Slowly but surely the United States, the USSR, Japan, and Canada will be drawn closer together by their growing awareness of their similarities and the common problems of their mammoth universities and colleges. Having few precedents to guide them, they must learn from each other through comparative study.

The disparity of senior-school attendance between these four mass education countries and Europe is extremely significant for understanding the inner workings of their tertiary system. One of the major contributions of recent studies in Paris by the Organization for Economic Cooperation and Development (OECD) has been the discovery that higher education enrollments are perfectly correlated with previous secondary-school enrollments. The increased number of secondary-school graduates is the tail that wags the dog of tertiary enrollments. Until Europe ceases to lag behind these four countries in senior secondary school enrollments, it will be unable to catch up in college and university enrollments. Meanwhile, today's high senior secondary enrollments in the USSR, Canada, and Japan will force vast higher education enrollments in these countries, thereby widening the gap between them and Europe and bringing them more into line with the United States. There is a mass "feel" about these countries. An experienced observer will predict without hesitation that they are destined to follow the achievements, though hopefully perhaps avoid the mistakes, of the United States.

But while Europe has lagged behind these other countries, it has not been deprived of an important comparative significance. Behind Europe lies the third world, where hopes and aspirations are not matched by reality and where schools, though all molded on European patterns, are less abundant and sometimes pitifully few. Europe, halfway between the two worlds, populous, industrial, and an early pioneer in mass education at the lower levels, is now taking steps to bring its higher education into line. In all countries of Europe, but particularly in the northwest the last decades have witnessed a spectacular expansion of enrollments. This process of catching up contains interesting lessons for countries moving fast toward modernity, such as Australia, New Zealand, China, Puerto Rico, or Turkey. Even in other countries in Africa, Latin America, and Asia, whose efforts are yet to be rewarded by spectacular growth, expansion problems will be made easier to solve by following precedents accumulated in advanced countries.

The explosion of postcompulsory schooling, half accomplished in mass education countries but only beginning in Europe, has placed the ancestress of university education in a position to learn from comparative analysis. Europeans tend to apply the term *mass* to increases in enrollment which while very large in terms of growth rates include only a minor proportion of the age groups compared with the leading mass education countries. By this use of the term, European conservatives can reconcile mass advances with their cherished elitist traditions for when mass is less than a quarter of the population, the level of ability remains high enough to permit expansion without reforming the syllabus. Deceptions of this kind can be avoided with the help of comparative analysis.

Serious studies of the degree of educational development of the world have already been made by men such as Harbison and Meyers (1964, 1965), Harbison, Maruhnic, and Resnick (1970), Curle (1964), and Garms (1969). The present volume attempts a cross-national assessment of the impact of innovations in higher education on industrial countries. The most significant of these innovations is enormous growth of enrollments. This book is a study of the reverberations and consequences of this eruption within North America, the USSR, and Japan in contrast to Europe. The major question it seeks to answer is: In copying the precedents of the United States, what are other mass education countries and Europe doing and what are the growing similarities and persistent differences in their attempts to streamline the world of higher education? The great advantage of a comparative approach is that it affords an analytical view of transnational intricacies of innovations and thus provides the broadest basis on which to build normative formulations.

Recognizing this need to study education in a comparative

perspective, the Organization for Economic Cooperation and Development (OECD) in Paris has sponsored a series of national studies of which volumes have so far been published or are due for publication for Britain (Burgess and Pratt, 1971; Perkin, 1969), France (Grignon and Passeron, 1970), Germany (Boning and Roeloffs, 1970), Yugoslavia (University of Zagreb, 1970), and Canada. *Universities for All* was originally expected to be a general synthesis of these volumes. But as the project progressed, it became apparent that its net must be cast much wider. The present report draws heavily on materials and enquiries prepared under the original OECD assignment, as well as on the remarkable collection of related studies which the OECD Secretariat has produced during the last few years and which are listed in the Bibliography. The present text, however, is more than a reproduction of the end-product of that assignment. It is an interpretation of a large body of facts and conclusions derived not only from most of the investigations of OECD concerning higher education, but also from my own knowledge and experience of higher education in the industrial countries of Europe, North America, USSR, and Japan. This immersion stems from familiarity with the languages of all of these countries and from teaching and lecturing in universities in each of them within the past decade, the most recent visits being to the USSR in 1967, to Japan in 1970, to various countries of Western Europe in 1970, 1971, and 1972, and to Canada in 1972.

This study specializes in these advanced nations. Continued comparative studies deserve to be made of other countries, and documentary coverage of industrialized countries beyond those studied here must be made more complete. Even for advanced countries, the generalizations and conclusions of this book must be recognized as tentative. Present-day comparative tools are grossly imperfect.

Three illustrations of difficulties familiar to comparative specialists will alert the reader to the reasons for the tentative nature of the conclusions. First, as the OECD and other international organizations are well aware, pitfalls are inherent in comparing statistics from official national sources. Statistical difficulties start with questioning the accuracy of numbers and end with disputing the appropriateness of categories. Europeans, for instance, often claim that in American university statistics, all freshmen and sophomores have to be discarded in making comparisons on the grounds that European graduates of the lycee and gymnasium are almost automatically accorded junior status in American colleges. As another example, a total picture of the volume of primary-school teacher training is not possible by comparing enrollments in *écoles normales* (secondary schools) in France, teacher training colleges (postsecondary colleges) in England, and faculties of education in American universities. Because such problems could not be solved without rigorous and lengthy comparative investigations, the present study has had to derive its general comparative notions from available traditional records.

Second, the tentative nature of the comparisons arises from substantive differences among countries and institutions. For example, in university systems with varied ability groups, fast changes are a natural part of innovation. Countries also respond differently to increased enrollments. Some that have doubled their student population manage to go on in the same way as before, while others that have not grown as much are convulsed by radical demands for change. Faculties, too, differ in their style of innovation. Science faculties, for example, are continuously evolving new curricula but seldom change their organization. In social science faculties, however, multiple change of curricula and organization is continuous. Thus it is virtually impossible to compare rates of innovation in Soviet universities (predominantly science) with English universities (predominantly humanities) and American universities (substantially social sciences).

Finally, the major cause for caution is the inability to use what this writer has elsewhere called the method of balanced comparison (Bereday, 1967). Under this method, the flow of materials from different countries is deliberately controlled to achieve a symmetrical confrontation. This means that, faced with available data in one country, the researcher is driven to produce equivalent data from other countries before comparison is attempted. No such procedure was, for the most part, possible in this study. This book has, rather, been written according to the method of illustrative comparison, namely, using materials whenever and wherever they happen to be available. The doubt attached to such imperfect comparative correspondence is not merely a matter of pedantry. Conclusions drawn from imperfectly balanced data facilitate the ever-present temptation to use comparative materials to support preconceived convictions.

An extremely detailed comparative study would have had to immerse itself in such intricacies. *Universities for All* has had to limit its methodological ambitions and content itself with the advantages of an appraisal from the inside and the outside by a European who is also an American and a specialist on Soviet and Japanese education.

This work has been financed by a substantive grant from the OECD and a supplementary grant from the Ford Foundation and has been indirectly contributed to by office facilities of Teachers College, Columbia University; Harvard University; and the University of Hawaii; and by travel funds of the U. S. Department of State. The list of people and institutions consulted all over the world is too vast to be given in detail. My special thanks are due to Ladislav Cerych and Dorotea Furth of the OECD, who acted generously and patiently as my contact men in the execution of this project and whose recent work (Cerych and Furth, 1972) anticipates some of the ideas in this book. My gratitude is also due to Harold Noah of Teachers College, Columbia University, and John Van de Graaff of the UNESCO Institute for Education in Hamburg for reading and commenting on parts of the manuscript. Amelia Augustus of New York acted as a valuable research associate for the latter parts of the book, while Susan Molmen of Honolulu helped with preliminaries. My assistants Sandra Anthony of Honolulu, Judith Guerra of New York and Honolulu, Irene Cook of Paris, Pierrina Andritsi of New York and Cambridge, and Corinne Murphy of Cambridge are to be warmly thanked for carrying the book through from the beginning to its final conclusion.

New York   GEORGE Z. F. BEREDAY
January 1973

Dedicated to Thaddeus Matthew Sigmund; Sigmund; Sigmund Marc; Wiley Ervine; Ronald George; Wiley Milan; Christopher Sigmund.

CONTENTS

UNIVERSITIES
FOR ALL

International Perspectives
on Mass Higher Education

WHERE DO REFORMS
TAKE US?

1

Fools, it is said, rush in where angels fear to tread. History will have to decide whether genius or madness caused Americans to gallop headlong into the age of mass higher education. While the pioneer trail is pursued swiftly by Canada, the USSR, and Japan, and only somewhat more cautiously by Europe, it is not unreasonable to ask why this extension of elite training is being indiscriminately undertaken. Masses of students have appeared, vast finances have been mobilized, and intricate higher education structures have been provided; but no one has stopped to ask about the reason for such efforts.

Nobody clearly knows what the concept of mass higher education will ultimately mean. As an ideal, it is possible to dream of an entire school system—a rectangle instead of the usual triangle or trapezoid—in which all human beings will find themselves from entrance to graduation without exclusion. It is possible to dream of a university in which a department for engineers will stand side by side with a department for plumbers, both instructed in their skill with the addition of a healthy dose of Plato. In practice, for the world as a whole, which is still 60 percent illiterate, even one year's universal schooling is an extremely ambitious objective. Even in most industrialized countries only eight years of schooling can be counted as universal because their senior secondary schools continue to be selective and elitist. If mass education countries are defined as those in which at least 75 percent of school-age youngsters complete senior secondary schooling after ten to twelve years of attendance, only the USA, Canada, and Japan exceed this mark today and only the USSR may do so soon. Few other countries have so far reached or are likely soon to reach even 50 percent. Thus, the designation of the USA, the USSR, Canada, and Japan as mass education countries is based on their high percentages of students who completed secondary education. If the reader will imagine school systems as stacks of children's blocks, he will see a bottom layer of 100-percent-compulsory blocks encompassing all children and common to all industrial countries, with a second layer of post-compulsory secondary blocks, which for the first four countries are more than half as wide (60 percent to 90 percent) and for European countries half as wide or less (25 percent to 50 percent).

In higher education proper, the contrast between Europe and the four mass education countries becomes less sharp. No country, not even the USA, enrolls more than 40 percent of the relevant age group in universities and colleges (though there are substantial statistical uncertainties about this percentage and about the 20 percent assigned to other advanced countries). In addition, few of the most advanced European countries (such as Sweden, which exceeds Japan) have much larger attendance percentages than has the rest of Europe. The university traditions of Japan and the USSR, and even more of Canada, are roughly half way between the European and USA patterns. Their organization is certainly European, and there is much historical and traditional affinity between them and the European universities. This statistical and organizational continuum makes a distinction between the mass higher education countries and Europe somewhat artificial.

Yet, again, a rather different "feel" about the Japanese and Soviet universities, and certainly about the Canadian universities, distinguishes them from the European universities and makes it not wholly inappropriate to group them with the US universities. The best of them are highly selective in admission, although Harvard and Yale are even more so. In countries with old university traditions, the secondary schools have grown downward as an extension of university cultural dominance (Organization for Economic Cooperation and Development, 1971, p. 35). In mass higher education countries, preuniversity schools seem to be growing upward from the extension of literacy to the masses of children (Bereday, 1969, p. 359). In these countries the universities are better prepared to incorporate technical streams and to foster continuity between secondary school programs and their own course sequences. Mass character is still only latent in the USSR, Canada, and Japan, but one senses it just under the surface, and these countries, unlike those in Europe, already have mass education at lower levels and are close to universal secondary education.

Thus, mass higher education countries are defined as those in which a spirit of universal attendance prevails, even though there is not always enough tenacity to enforce this spirit. It is in the USA, the USSR, Canada, and Japan that the notions of academic elitism have been most seriously weakened. These countries are close to admitting the desirability of universal access to college, though none of them puts this belief fully into practice.

In any event, the term "access to college" (or to some other form of the traditional sixteen years of schooling) may shortly be losing its meaning for those countries. Advances in technology may serve to disseminate knowledge in highly unorthodox fashion through television, through computers, through flying teachers, and individualized home study. It would perhaps be more appropriate to say that mass higher education exists where everybody "pursues" education for sixteen years without necessarily attending schools.

Not even the United States has adopted the concept of mass education as an ideal of untrammeled pursuit of education by all, and other countries are unlikely to embrace the concept completely. (There is a substantial gap between the aspirations and fears of university reformers everywhere and the lengths to which they will go in practice.) Yet the American model of mass education has sometimes too unthinkingly become the object of reform aspirations abroad. Americans are rich and powerful and they wear blue jeans and drink Coca-Cola, but wearing blue jeans and drinking Coke do not automatically make other nations rich. The seeds for the true strengths, as well as the defects, of American society came from Europe but blossomed because the new soil was favorable. In re-importing their offshoots, other countries will no doubt develop different and distinctive adaptations. Our task here is to attempt to predict how these innovations elsewhere are likely to follow or di-verge from American patterns.

Characteristics of Reform

Universities everywhere are bastions of cultural stability and if left undisturbed become set in their ways; sudden change from such an entrenched static situation can be soul-wrenching. Each country has developed its own style for coping with this challenge. The notion in the USA that change is natural is different from the zigzag advances and reversals of Soviet policy. The Japanese magic mixture of reluctant traditionalism and enthusiastic modernization contrasts with a sense of natural development in Canada. Looking at European higher education today, historians may feel they have been there before: reflected there are all the themes that have de-veloped in mass countries. Europe is on the threshold of developing its own style. Its closest affinities are with the USA and Canada, but the urgencies it faces are those already confronted by the Japa-nese and the Soviets.

In the history of European higher education, as in the lower levels of education, change and innovation have not been sporadic. Women can now go to Oxford, though they had to wait several years after even Catholics were admitted, and Latin is no longer an ironclad entrance requirement. Bonn no longer has several chairs of Oriental studies while having only one in sociology. Even the academic study of education, that staggeringly beautiful but intel-lectually anemic Cinderella, has married her prince. The process begun by the humble teacher-training schools has ended with the establishment of chairs of education in the universities. Innovation in Europe today is no novelty. What is new is its convulsive nature. There is a tension in the air in Paris, Berlin, and Madrid that Mos-cow and Tokyo have known for some time.

Human institutions can be renovated in two ways. The first is by simple burgeoning. Throughout university history in Europe and in mass education countries quiet growth has been the main feature despite sudden bursts of reform. Universities of great eminence such as Oxford have often officially condemned expansion. Yet their student populations have doubled every quarter of a century. Science has long been kept down or altogether excluded, and yet technical universities in Germany and Russia have been almost effortlessly acquiring university status. The *grandes écoles* in France today enjoy a higher status than and jealously protect their independence from the universities which originally refused to accept them into the academic world. The junior colleges of Japan imperceptibly arose to take care of women's education. In England humble Owens College grew into the University of Manchester. Small, unknown towns in the United States became, in a matter of years, flourishing university towns. Strange subjects, cultivated by a Society of Apothecaries here or a Louis Pasteur there, became in time venerated fields of university learning. Unobtrusive, natural innovations occur and keep on occurring whenever groups of men take common counsel to change a curriculum, add a subject of study, or appoint a professor with more than orthodox vision. There is often debate at such meetings, but its tone is subdued.

The other type of renovation is less quiescent. Development, instead of being gradual, comes in sudden bursts, often by fits and starts. Change, or even the threat of change, sends convulsions through the system. Both the attackers of the old system and its defenders are agitated by violent feelings. This intensity is precisely the novel aspect in rapidly expanding university systems. Never before have Europeans been quite so agitated about reforms in higher education. Never before has the process of innovation in Japan been so intensely political. In England even Cardinal Newman would be surprised at the depth of introspection and self-study engaged in by contemporary universities. Fast, provocative, and direct change has been added to the quiet innovations which are still going on. The pressures that were handled relatively calmly in the USA and Canada and more roughly accommodated in the USSR and Japan are the same as those with which Europe now contends (see Bereday, 1972a).

The first common factor in university reform is the intensity with which young people in that portion of the intelligence curve traditionally deemed unsuitable for university education are now demanding it. As it becomes apparent that the old notions of ability are socially loaded and that widening the range of talent diversifies standards without necessarily lowering them, a lively battle is joined on the issue of liberalizing university admission. This battle is evident particularly in the USSR, Japan, and Europe. European universities are aghast at the impressive percentages of the relevant age group which pass through university gates in the United States and will no doubt soon do so in Japan, Canada, and the USSR. These three countries envisage university education for a third of their youth, whereas in Europe the prospect of one-sixth raises blood pressures to apoplectic levels in both advocates and opponents of reform. *Liberta d'accesso,* the freedom of access recently granted in Italy, appeals to the government and the political parties but hardly to all, or even most, of the alumni and professors. In the USSR and Japan, in which three-quarters of the relevant age group graduates from secondary schools but only about one-quarter is permitted to continue in the universities, the tensions generated by this bottleneck have been formidable.

How many to admit is one part of the question. Whom to choose among all those who clamor for entry is the second part. In all countries, even in the USSR, more than half the university places go to children of the high-status families, who are rarely more than 20 percent of the population. This well-known sociological fact has received much publicity, followed as usual, alas, by too little action. Entrance to universities even in industrial countries is so restricted that some of the social drive for wide entrance is bound to be diverted into condemnation of hereditary university education. Social justice in educational selection, however, is no easy matter. The fact that the children of the well-to-do score highly on almost any entrance test makes it difficult to dislodge them. Very few critics have so far suggested admission by lottery, as recently tried by a few colleges in America. But the odium against *les Heritiers,* the socially privileged students who are said to succeed intellectually because the tests themselves are biased in their favor, is increasing. The emerging question in higher education everywhere is what priority to assign to the bright sons of the poor. We would not be far off the mark to look at the whole question of innovation in mass higher education from the viewpoint of the admission gate.

The next common factor is the Horatio Alger ideal, which now affects and attracts not only individuals but institutions. In the old days, the problem was simply how to get into a university; now another problem has been added: how to become a university. Several new universities, such as Stirling in Scotland and Regensburg in Germany, have been created on the initiative or with the approval of existing universities. But the ambition of some nonuniversity institutions is another matter. They can no longer be kept in their place by simple sneers at their ridiculous pretentions. The twilight zone of minor colleges and institutions which train teachers or technicians is demanding academic recognition, partial at first, but ultimately complete. In the older dual systems of education, the teaching body of these institutions came from a lesser world, holding vocational diplomas or, at best, clutching the hard-earned evening school baccalaureate or *Abitur*. Now they are likely to be alumni of their own institutions or college men chafing under a sense of inferiority. From a National College of Horology in England to a *Pädagogische Hochschule* in Germany, their theme song is the same —they rail against the intellectual elitists, the *Philologen*, who deny them equality.

Various means are being tried to satisfy their ambitions or to thwart them. *Zweiter Weg,* the second route to the university via senior vocational schools, seems to hold out promise of inclusion; binary systems, a parallel build-up of universities and post-secondary vocational schools, promise equivalence instead. But those who opt for the latter will soon demand the former. After the Second World War, American occupation authorities pressured Japan into converting more than two hundred teacher-training colleges and minor institutions into universities. One can easily imagine the consternation of the seventeen Imperial universities when confronted with this apparition. Established universities everywhere and especially in Europe, where they are most established, are sooner or later due for a similar shock.

Next, widening the gates of higher education and adding new gates have affected ancient academic structures. University government has had to adjust to new men and new institutions. The main thrust and the greatest shock are experienced internally in the attempt to deprive chairholders of their power. Like the guilds from which they spring, the universities are not democracies but republics. Professors are said to behave like so many doges of Venice, as absolute and conservative rulers. But a true republic of princes, a pure self-government of teachers, survives in few institutions. Only places such as Oxford continue to be governed by hebdomadal councils of professors and heads of colleges, elected to the vice-chancellorship in rotation. Elsewhere, universities have had to surrender some of their prerogatives to the state, the church, the cities, or other financing organizations. But this surrender is no longer enough. The right of professors to be consulted on all university decisions is so vast and their powers of veto so extensively used that they, who should be and sometimes are the most liberal of all men, have come under suspicion. Converting the university structure based on chairs into one based on departments has been the answer in several countries. The USA as originator of the system and Japan and Canada as the first to adopt it have developed the common model.

Such conversion has not exempted even these countries from criticism. All universities are bitterly taunted for going through a period of decline. Many say that the political atmosphere within the universities is unhealthy. Where there is no inertia, intrigues have taken its place. Decision-making has degenerated into die-hard stands and power politics. Subtle games of social or intellectual snobbery often contain one group while protecting another. Alliances by age have elevated the latent rebellion of youth against adults to the status of an open social phenomenon. Two new war cries, junior staff power and student power, have been widely recognized; they may very soon become a reality.

Yet another tremor shaking the mass university system may well bring down the ivory tower in ruins. Outside the university walls, public opinion has been insisting on partnership in determining university affairs. Most public leaders today are university graduates, but their loyalty as alumni seems outweighed by their irritation with the decay of their alma mater. The enlarged scope of university education calls for increased support from the public purse. The cry of "no taxation without representation" is heard everywhere from laymen standing outside the gates. Now that the British universities have had to agree to government audit, even those unique bastions of university independence seem to be abandoning the principle of public support with no strings attached. University strongholds have always been buffeted by the winds of political and social doctrine. The whole principle of lofty isolation must now yield to a concept of partnership between the university and the public. This concept cannot fail to speed change, though often causing a lack of long-range vision. In a sense *Lernfreiheit*, freedom to study as one pleases, may undermine *Lehrfreiheit*, the freedom of the teaching body to stand fast in the midst of change. Attacks on academic tenure are increasing. The first reform of this kind has already appeared in the USSR in the form of quinquennial review and reappointment.

Although each country gives its particular flavor to reforms, Europe shares with the mass education countries the fourfold shock treatment it is experiencing. As in Europe, the American multiversity must contend with outside pressure for mass admissions. Like the old English universities, the august Japanese imperial universities must now learn to live on terms of equality with a host of teacher-training schools elevated to academic rank. Universities in the USSR and Canada, like those in other countries, must reckon with internal pressures from students and young intellectuals. All industrial countries must mobilize to defend themselves against outside interference by the patriots, the rich, the party dogmatists, or the nationalists.

But two lines of reform with which the mass universities in the USA, Canada, the USSR, and Japan have had to contend seem to have less importance in Europe. First, in Europe fights about university structure have overshadowed the campaign for curricular change. Curricular reforms in Europe have been hotly debated, and many bold and creative attempts have been made to introduce them. But even the striking innovations in the otherwise conservative Italian university curricula, the *liberta dei studii*, amount to free choice among existing subjects in one subject faculty rather than the addition of new subjects. The lesson furnished by the pioneering introduction of elective subjects at Harvard, sponsored by President Charles Eliot, has been only partly heeded. The European universities, reluctant to allow tailor-made curricula even in established subjects such as law or philosophy are under little pressure to add to their degree subjects, even more outlandish courses like bull-breeding or bowling. Few experiment with new teaching methods. No Paul Goodman or Marshall McLuhan has clouded the scene. Old traditions still persist of what is and what is not appropriate within university walls.

New subjects are brought into the universities only by being championed by those special-interest institutions seeking university status. Even so, the subjects they champion, such as business training, nursing, or social welfare, have a long way to go before they are considered, let alone accepted, by the universities. Other curricular questions are for the most part ignored. Issues such as polytechnization in the Soviet universities, general education courses in Japanese universities, or summer study in American universities are not debated. Case study methods versus lectures in American law schools, twin major instead of single major in Soviet pedagogical institutes, junior college versus university courses for women in Japan—these debates indicate curricular awareness outside Europe. By comparison Europe is taking halting steps: several new universities in France and in other countries now advocate seminars in preference to lectures, which still dominate elsewhere; a four-year instead of a three-year course at Keele inaugurated interdisciplinary requirements for students of both sciences and humanities, and curricular experimentation is taking place in other new English universities; the Italian and Spanish reforms of higher education include curricular elements that are worth watching. But the tone of these movements is subdued; compared with the battles over access or structure they are insignificant.

A second major difference between the mass education countries and Europe lies in the comparative importance attached to research, teaching and public service. While European professors are criticized for doing too little research in the universities, in the USA criticism of the compulsive tyranny of faculty research and of the affluent, research-minded, absentee professor has reached formidable proportions. The abandonment of undergraduate teaching to tutors, themselves usually mere graduate students, is deplored. Grantsmanship and promotion to full rank solely on the record of publications are pointed out as devices to lure good teachers away from teaching. The American university is perceptibly being impelled to become not a community of research scholars but a post-secondary teaching school. Anyone who has watched at secondary level even such an innocuous transformation as that of the Boston Latin School into a public high school can sense the coming change at the higher level from the academy to mass university.

The *collegium* survives in American universities mostly in the bull sessions held in common rooms or students' dormitories. Elsewhere, it exists in graduate schools, where doctoral students and their advisers still attempt to recreate Socratic discourse. Scholarly disputations and research are increasingly looking for a safe harbor within research institutes, which eventually may be pushed out of the universities altogether. Places such as the Institute of Advanced Studies at Princeton, the center at Aspen, or the "Think Tank" at Stanford, where distinguished faculties gather for full-time research, have no students, thus turning into a trend the precedents established by All Souls College and Nuffield College in Oxford. The *College de France,* a forum of learned men without students, has few counterparts in France, but in the Soviet Union a whole series of academies and institutes, which live (and train advanced students) entirely outside the universities, has multiplied. In Japan, the research sections of ministries and national institutes for research in various fields, by no means unique in this respect, have far better staffs and publications than many a university. A demarcation line is visible in the USA between mass universities, with their many teaching faculties but poor publication records, and the few highly placed universities at which research and expertise overshadow teaching. Few problems of this kind have arisen in Europe, where the research obligation of the teaching staff has never been strong.

Similarly, there is no striking expansion in the extramural activities of European universities in the allied fields of community service and political participation. Community service has never been a major concern of universities in Europe, in comparison with some extra-European countries (and the USSR)', where fully integrated university correspondence-course departments have been established. The British Open University may lead to a striking innovation in teaching by television, but it has much to learn from the mature and tested precedents in Japan. Many British and other universities have also established extramural departments catering to outsiders, but they lack the scope and vigor of their American or for that matter Australian counterparts.

As for political participation, the academic world in the West has castigated German universities for failing to take a stand against Hitler's takeover (Lilge, 1948; Ringer, 1969). But the European universities still take relatively less interest than the mass institutions in political life outside the academy. Even in France, *la republique des professeurs,* where intellectuals are listened to, and in Italy, where professors have a virtual monopoly of cabinet posts, universities are nonpolitical. Demonstrations and demands by young people constantly repeat these accusations; but students lack the force to institute changes even in countries of turbulent student protest, such as Japan. As regards political activism of the universities, Europe is worse off than the mass education countries; in fact, it is in some ways more restricted than the USSR, where even the severely controlled universities vigorously engage in approved political activism. The power of the teaching body and students in Europe cannot be compared with that in the USA, where the political opinion of university people, the teachers especially, has influence far out of proportion to their numbers.

Enlarged admission, institutional upgrading, internal restructuring, and external cogovernment are areas of innovation which might be described as hard reforms, while curricular change and the place of teaching, research, and community service are soft reforms. In Europe hard reforms overshadow soft reforms, whereas in the four major mass higher education countries the reverse is more common.

This contrast provides a clue to the emerging typology of reforms. Mass movements in higher education seem to have two stages. At the beginning, problems of university entrance loom large and pressure at the admission gate dominates the scene. Since universities nearly always resist the masses, the masses must first assault the structure itself. Rivals to the old universities must be created to challenge their monopoly. The internal hold on decision-making must be democratized to ensure a liberal admissions policy. Outside society must be mobilized to compel compliance and to hold vigil over the continued fair play of the academic community.

Once the masses are within the university they turn their

attention to other issues: curriculum, relevance of content, and the methods of presentation. A forceful appeal is also made to the teaching body to render direct service. Their research function must now be made subordinate to or integrated with their roles as teachers inside the academic walls and as makers of public opinion outside.

European higher education reforms are still in the first stage. Only after the university structure is adapted to mass needs and content of instruction becomes more important than questions of admission will the second stage, now exemplified by American, Canadian, Japanese, and Soviet universities, make its appearance.

The same point can be expressed differently by surveying the whole span of the development of universities. In medieval times and up to the industrial revolution universities responded to what might be called an administrative need. Apart from medical practitioners, the universities were devoted to the production of the verbal elite—scholars, clerics, lawyers, and civil servants. In this phase the structure of the universities and the community of scholars were established. Since, in terms of social class, scholars nestled between the clergy and the rising third estate, their style was partly that of cathedral chapters and partly that of trade guilds.

The second phase of university development spans the time from the industrial revolution to the Second World War. During this period, universities were asked to serve professional needs. Development of a wide range of skilled personnel, from army officers to accountants, from anthropologists to biochemists, was brought within their purview. The function of the university was to train an enlarged elite. As the high-level specialties of a technological society expanded, so did the variety of degree subjects, the numbers of teachers and students, and the intricacies of organization.

The third phase, beginning in the middle of this century, grew naturally out of the second. Universities are now forced to move toward training perhaps the majority, if not the whole, of the young-adult age groups. They seem likely to be made systematically responsible for preparing students for all or most of the complicated tasks required in highly industrialized modern life. They may try further diversification. Or they may attempt to consolidate programs covering the basic subjects, leaving specialization to courses given by industry or other forms of on-the-job training. The teaching staff

required to man such a higher education enterprise will no longer
be able to combine the contemplative, teaching, and research qualities of old-style university professors. The conflict between the functions of the university as a school, a research center, and a maker
of public opinion must be resolved or accommodated. We have
already seen that the major thrust today is in the direction of the
university as a school.

On this historical continuum, European universities are in
transition from the second phase to the third, though they are still
primarily in the second. The countries of mass higher education are
firmly in the latter stage. Previously, Europe was always the major
innovator and leader in university reform, but now the reforms,
although bearing the national stamp and the common European
style, in reality reprodurce the trends already established in Japan,
the USSR, and North America.

Dynamics of Reform

The precedents established by the mass education countries
not only suggest the direction of reforms in Europe and all the modernizing countries but also enable us to dismiss the question whether
such evolution is desirable—for it is inevitable. Everywhere in the
world, higher education is reforming itself only because it is under
pressure. Occasionally this pressure may come from outside, as when
the British and the Americans artificially increased the production
of technologists to match the unnerving production of Soviet scien-
tists. Often the pressure is internal, from people who have learned
that a college education pays. Nothing in the history of universities
suggests that the pressure will abate until all objectives are achieved.
Higher education systems merely have the options of resisting and
delaying the change as long as politically possible or of taking the
sting out of pressures for reform by anticipating them and by ad-
justing to them. In the disunited and widely disparate European
academic world as in the pluralistic milieu of large industrial countries, no doubt both choices will be tried in turn.

All advanced systems develop on similar lines, but they do
not necessarily arrive at the same destination. Judging from present
trends in European innovations and from reform precedents in mass

education countries, we can predict that circumstances in each country are likely to produce different solutions.

Among countries with mass education, two distinct modes of operation have emerged. One, represented by the USA and Canada, is a grass-roots system; the other, represented by Japan and the USSR, is a guided system. In the former, innovation is permitted to arise from internal pressure from below: grass grows where conditions favor it, albeit occasionally aided by the gardener. This system has a great variety of institutions and degree subjects. Any uniformity is a product of fashion—is voluntarily copied. In this laissez-faire system, nothing is done until a group of citizens is formed to do it. Authorities may assist and quicken growth; they seldom, if ever, initiate it. The grass-roots system affords maximum flexibility while it permits deviations from earlier patterns of excellence and high standards. The guided system, in contrast, is characterized by counsel from above; expansions and modification are undertaken not primarily in response to pressure from below but because of overall considerations of the common good. Such considerations often mean that the sometimes reluctant or uninstructed population must be persuaded or even compelled. The guided system, by reflecting the values of those who guide it, avoids the gross perversions of the grass-roots system, but it lacks some of the latter's spontaneity and diversity; it prefers discipline to flexibility, rigor to vigor.

The countries of mass higher education use different methods but share a similar destination. But the European system stands a good chance of developing a hybrid pattern of its own. Europe may not move as far toward mass education as the others have done. Their cultures are newer—formed by colonization in North America, by revolution in USSR, and by modernization in Japan. Social barriers are fewer and the net of educational opportunity may be cast wider and further than in Europe. The hybridized European pattern may rather take the form of a union between intellectual elitism and mass opportunity. The California university system is one expression of such union in which universal access is balanced with rewards for high achievement, rather along the lines once proposed by Thomas Jefferson for education in Virginia. Europe, or parts of it, may well evolve a university system which will satisfy ambitions sufficiently to relieve social tension from below and will therefore be free to retain certain selected features of the elite system above. In terms of numbers, while the mass education countries now aim at college education for half their populations, Europe may perhaps be able to establish a structure catering to one-quarter of the population. In terms of institutional structure, the Soviet Union has combined a limited number of universities with a vast number of specialized single-discipline institutions. Perhaps a modification of this pattern will permit Europe to create a balanced institutional network.

Whether or not Europe arrives at a full mass system, it can blend the features of the grass-roots and the guided systems. The variety and multiple aspirations of the European nations, the differences of religious faith and regional culture have long found expression in a variety of institutions with distinct missions. At the same time, European higher education has relied on central direction, including the predetermination of curricula and financial control over buildings and staffing. The conditions thus exist for a hybrid system. In the USA it is fashionable to characterize the schools as possessing diversity within unity. In reality there is little unity other than spiritual. This characterization may more properly be reserved for the emerging reformed European universities if they succeed in once again balancing old traditions and modernity.

In assessing the dynamism of reformed university institutions, we may ask: Will the academic changes now taking place lead to a new stability, or will the new structure, confronted with a constantly moving society, never reach equilibrium? Must not the universities resign themselves to being permanently in flux? Should university standards, practices, and procedures shift from a fixed and now untenable position to a new point, better adapted to contemporary needs, but still fixed? Or should higher education simply be a meeting zone of men and ideas unbound by structure or convention, flexible and indeterminate? Nobody knows the answers, but sufficiently clear comparative patterns are already emerging to allow at least some tentative prediction of future developments. Comparison of the guided systems and those based on the grass-roots approach is revealing. In the guided systems, innovation is viewed as a filmstrip, in the grass-roots systems as a film. Japan and the USSR attempt to reach a series of stationary conditions through change. As with the stills in a filmstrip, the eye moves from one static picture to the next. In a sense, a filmstrip and a film are the same, but the speed of film conveys to the eye not a sequence of stills but a sense of movement. The patterns of life of universities in the USA, and to some extent in Canada, in contrast with those in the USSR and Japan, seem more like perpetual motion.

Evaluating the power of these differing styles of innovation is difficult. Under the pressure of modernity, the Soviet system has been remarkably successful in absorbing shocks and in adapting to shifting needs by adopting a series of static positions. But Japan has not been equally successful. As the wave of student riots which threatened to bring academic life to a standstill suggests, the Japanese filmstrip has not been moving fast enough to suit Japanese conditions. Thus, Japan is under pressure to move further in the direction of American flexibility. But oddly enough, the United States has also been under pressure from the young to move even faster. The worlds of higher education in Japan, Canada, and the USA are likely to resemble each other more closely with the passage of time. Impelled by the relentless logic of the technocratic age, these countries may never be permitted the luxury of a series of stabilities.

Traditional academic habits in Europe may have the same stabilizing effect that Soviet ideology has had. Europe may be able to join the mass higher education club less tempestuously by going through bursts of innovation alternating with calm periods of consolidation. In the USSR the most recent period of consolidation began in the mid-1960s after a wave of change had swept the system during the preceding decade. But in Europe, the whole of the 1960s was a period during which the dikes were being washed away, and the rising tide must spend itself before academic life in Europe can resume a calm state. While the Soviet Union is consolidating and Europe exploding, their North American and Japanese counterparts are evolving incessantly. A two-step dynamic of reform is once more suggested. In world overview, countries with elitist higher education can afford the luxury of alternating reform with stabilization, but no such remedy is available once mass enrollment in higher education is reached. Such judgment may displease conservative academicians, but others may welcome the fact that higher education is on the verge of giving more people more opportunities to follow more individualized paths toward academic excellence.

POSTCOMPULSORY
NOT
POSTSECONDARY

2

Mass education countries and Europe have been the victims of an enrollment explosion under whose impact they must shed not only some established ways of training academics and some modes of academic thought, but also some of their academic accounting. There is little good reason to cling exclusively to established systems of gathering and presenting educational statistics. The distinction between primary, secondary, and postsecondary enrollments still made by all industrial countries is a legacy from an earlier age when primary statistics were a measure of mass literacy, secondary statistics of the formation of clerical class, and university statistics of the members of the intellectual elite. The technological age has lessened the relevance of such statistics. As vast masses of the population spend a longer time at school, and as young adults as well as teenagers specialize with increasing diversity, only a limited purpose can be served by splitting the statistics of postcompulsory education into secondary and postsecondary education. As mentioned earlier, future higher education enrollments can best be predicted by present secondary enrollments. Elitism in education and wholly vocational orientation begin where compulsory education ends. The gap between the university education and senior secondary schooling is rapidly narrowed. In these circumstances little is gained by clinging to an almost illusory line of transition at the age of eighteen.

Enrollment Explosion

Conventional statistics retain, of course, their traditional uses. The extremely rapid increase in higher education as shown in a recent report (OECD, 1971e) is a phenomenon common to almost all countries and can be illustrated by any set of figures. During the past fifteen years, of the twenty-three countries under OECD review, six (including Canada and Sweden) experienced tripled enrollments and several others doubled theirs. The growth in absolute numbers has put a heavy strain on higher education facilities in all industrial countries. The total number of higher education students (both university and nonuniversity) in all OECD countries (Europe, the USA, Japan, and Canada) was 4,700,000 in 1955–1956 and 12,500,000 in 1968–1969. In 1968, adding the USSR, the totals were respectively 6,500,000 and 17,000,000. A majority of these students were in fact in the four mass systems: student population in these countries increased from 5.26 million in 1955 to 13.4 million in 1968. The totals for Europe alone were in round numbers 1.3 million in 1955–1956 and 3.5 million in 1968–1969. A specially important fact, however, as far as Europe is concerned is that not only numbers were increasing but the rate of increase has been speeding up. Faced with normal increases, higher education systems can function normally, but unusual increases call for emergency measures.

Enrollment figures have a threefold significance for innovation. First, in absolute terms the sheer rise of student numbers is likely to compel expanded facilities. The increase in student population is thus a sure index of the "effort" each country has made and must immediately make to cope with pressures. Increased enrollment, even where it does not cause innovations, at least means more buildings and more teachers. A larger share of resources, probably urgently needed elsewhere, must be deflected to education.

A second aspect of enrollment increases is that in most countries they were accompanied until recently by a deteriorating student success rate. If the graduation ratio were to continue to decline, in the long run social costs would change in the following manner: expanding intake would mean that the frustrations of those refused admission would be replaced by concern about dropouts. The USSR, Japan, and Europe may have to cope with the problems of large numbers of people with an unfinished college education in the manner of the "failed B.A.," long familiar in India. The remedy among mass education countries would be either to attack the stiffness of graduation requirements, permitting more diversified success for people with less than orthodox scholarly talents, as has been the case in the United States; or to hold these requirements constant while capitalizing on the rise of academic comprehension in an intergenerational sense. The explosion of enrollments in France suggests that if graduation standards are not progressively stiffened, an increased number of people in each successive generation will be capable of negotiating them successfully.

Third, enrollment figures of different countries must be compared in relation to relevant age groups, because only these figures provide a precise picture of the opportunities for higher study that have become available to the population. The relative width of admissions is the main factor behind pressures for reform. In this respect, the record of Europe in comparison with the mass education countries is not impressive. Figure 1* shows that, among the mass

* Sources: USA: *Digest of Educational Statistics—1970.* Washington, D.C.: National Center of Education Statistics, Department of Health, Education and Welfare, p. 4. CANADA: *Estimated Participation Rates in Canadian Education 1968–69—Statistics of Canada.* Ottawa, 1972, p. 162. JAPAN: *Educational Standards in Japan—1970.* Ministry of Education, Government of Japan, March 1971. USSR: *Statistical Yearbook.* Paris: UNESCO, 1970. GERMANY: *Bevölkerung und Kultur—Statistisches.* Wiesbaden: Bundesamt, 1970. FRANCE: *Tableaux de l'education nationale. Statistiques. Retrospectives—1958–68.* Paris: Ministere de le'education national, 1971. ITALY: *Annuario Statistico dell'Istruzione Italiana.* Rome: Istituto Centrale di Statistica, 1970; and *Statistical Yearbook.* Paris: UNESCO, 1970. UNITED KINGDOM: *Statistics of Education—1969.* Vols. 1, 3, 4, and 6 (England and Wales only). London: H.M.S.O., 1970. SWEDEN: *Statistisk Arsbok.* Stockholm: National Central Bureau of Statistics, 1971

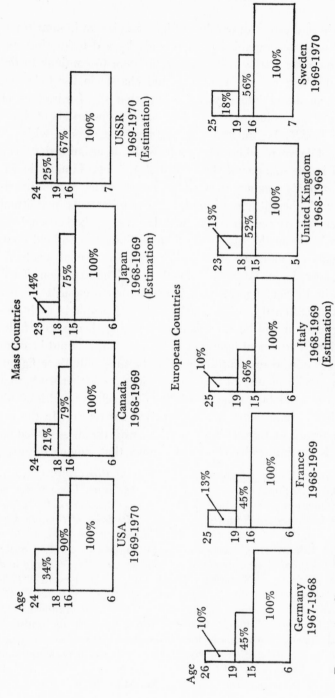

FIGURE 1. Comparison of senior secondary and postsecondary attendance in mass higher education countries and European countries, by percentages of age group. Prepared by Jean-Pierre Pellegrin, Organization for Cooperation and Development. The error of using different years when appropriate is smaller than when making an adjustment.

education countries, only Japan enrolls as few as 14 percent of college-age youth, roughly the same percentage as that shown for all the foremost European countries. Japan makes up for this deficiency by a very high enrollment ratio of senior secondary students, namely three-quarters of the whole age group. It can safely be predicted that the explosion of numbers in the universities in Japan is imminent. Other mass education countries, with the USA at 34 percent, Canada at 21 percent, and the USSR at 25 percent, have a ten- to twenty-point lead over the Europeans in postsecondary enrollments.

The figures reflect the disparity between efforts in higher education in Europe and those in its mass education rivals. With a total population of 560 million, the USA, the USSR, Canada, and Japan provided higher education for 13.4 million in 1968; with a population of 360 million, Europe provided higher education for 3.6 million. Stated another way, in mass education countries one-fortieth of the population was receiving higher education in 1968 while in Europe the fraction was only one-hundredth. OECD statistics demonstrate that economic growth does not cause uniform subsequent expansion of higher education enrollment in all countries. But since the power and the wealth of the mass education countries are self-evident, there may be a reverse relation of cause and effect between the volume of higher education and the subsequent growth of economic potential. This economic potential provides the financial basis for innovation. Increased enrollment means a wider spread of ability and therefore more flexible programs. The presence in the universities of a diversified population with varied social backgrounds and political allegiances must mean increased potential for reform.

Europe's leap forward in enrollments may be due to its initial low position. Future innovations depend on long-term growth rates. Very roughly speaking, the major European countries have just passed the higher education enrollment ratio of 10 percent. A few countries, such as Sweden, the UK, and France, have about a three- to five-point lead over the others. The average annual growth rate of enrollments in Europe from 1960 to 1965 was 8.5 percent, approximately double that of the preceding decade.

Two alternate growth patterns are possible in Europe. One is the rather unlikely prospect that the expansion rate will be substantially arrested. In this event, a regular machinery for absorbing increases in student population would soon come into being, and the state of emergency in higher education would cease to exist. There is some evidence that countries with a very high growth rate in one period experience a slowdown in the next period. As an "optimum" student population is reached, growth rates may universally become stable or even decline. No one at present envisages such stabilization, though some circles are certainly whispering about it. But if this leveling off should occur, the present bulge in enrollments will appear to have been a temporary emergency, and measures taken to meet it will historically have been no more than makeshift.

The more likely possibility is that growth rates will continue to rise. With present higher education enrollment of 10 percent or more of the age group and a stable increase close to 8 percent per annum, it would take a whole decade for Europe to exceed 20 percent enrollment and a second decade to approach the present USA percentage. By then, forecasters in some of the mass education countries envisage 75 percent of or even all college-age students attending higher education institutions. Even if Europe should accept a low ratio as optimum and should succeed in stabilizing at a low figure, quite convulsive expansion must still be expected, and what has happened so far seems to be merely a beginning.

Postcompulsory Statistics

The absolute size of the student population and its size in comparison to the nonstudent population are both causes of change and incitements to resist change. The dynamism, or lack of it, in the European system, as will be seen in the next chapter, also depends on the distribution of students by social class, sex, and subjects of study. But the size and nature of enrollments, while having an impact on innovations, is itself an innovation. The force of this impact should be determined with the greatest possible precision.

Table 1 gives the orthodox picture of absolute enrollments in the relevant countries for 1967–1968 in relation to the total population. This picture does not tell us as much as it should. The proportion of the population which has the opportunity to acquire

Table 1

PROPORTION OF STUDENTS IN THE TOTAL POPULATION

Country	Population	Student Population	Student Population as Percent of Population
Finland	4,689,000	65,000[a]	1.39%
Sweden	7,912,000	107,000	1.35
France	49,915,000	637,000	1.28
Denmark	4,870,000	61,400	1.26
Netherlands	12,725,000	140,000[a]	1.10
Yugoslavia	20,154,000	211,000	1.05
Belgium	9,619,000	98,000[a]	1.02
Italy	53,798,000	521,000	0.97
United Kingdom	55,391,000	530,000	0.96
Norway	3,819,000	35,000[a]	0.92
Greece	8,803,000	73,500	0.83
Austria	7,350,000	52,800	0.72
Ireland	2,910,000	21,000[a]	0.72
Switzerland	6,145,000	44,100	0.72
Spain	32,622,000	229,000[a]	0.70
Germany	60,184,000	396,000	0.66
Iceland	201,000	1,300	0.65
Luxembourg	336,000	1,700	0.51
Portugal	9,497,000	42,000	0.44
Turkey	33,540,000	120,000[a]	0.36
USA	201,152,000	6,391,000	3.18
Canada	20,772,000	420,000[a]	2.02
USSR	237,800,000	4,311,000	1.81
Japan	101,090,000	1,395,000	1.38

[a] Estimation.

SOURCES: *United Nations Demographic Yearbook 1968.* New York: Statistical office of the United Nations, 1968. *Development of Higher Education, 1950–67, Statistical Survey.* Paris: OECD, 1970.

higher education is very unequal from country to country, even
in Europe. The differences between Finland, Sweden, Denmark,
France, and the Netherlands on the one hand and Portugal and
Turkey on the other suggest a gap between developed and underdeveloped countries. When European higher education figures are
compared with those of the mass education countries it is obvious
that the percentages for these countries begin where European percentages end. The only exception, Finland, may be due to a blend
of European and Soviet influences on its educational practices.

In comparing different countries, we are obviously also dealing with different orders of magnitude. Even where the higher education enrollment ratios are similar, as they are for Sweden and Japan, the sheer differences in size mean the difference between
small-scale production and mass production. The life of a university,
like the life of an industry, is colored by its size. Size imprints itself
on institutions and on higher education systems as it does on whole
nations. These differences in bulk limit the significance of comparing the mass education countries with individual European countries on a national scale. It would be better to compare each of the
mass education countries with Europe as a whole or to take the individual states of the United States, the provinces of Canada, the
Soviet republics, or the Japanese prefectures as standards for single-
country analysis.

Mere size has other consequences, too: consumption of books
and cost of buildings, on the one hand, and social prestige and curricular traditionalism, on the other, are bound to be significantly
affected by mass. To cite another effect, the sheer size of a country
compels adequate geographic coverage. In Europe, the home of the
wandering scholar and the residential college, "neighborhood colleges" have a short tradition. Until recently, there has been no ur-
gency to expand their numbers because poor students, who are most
likely to benefit from them, were a small minority. The increase in
student numbers has forced countries to fill in the blanks in their
higher education maps and to improve the opportunities for those
unable or unwilling to travel. General national statistics scarcely reflect such concerns and therefore do not give the best picture of the
size of the student flow through the universities.

Let us now look closely at the proportions of higher education students not in the total population but in the population of the age group from which these students are recruited. The OECD statistics, as shown in Table 2, use a standard method of computing

Table 2
PROPORTION OF HIGHER-EDUCATION STUDENTS IN TOTAL
TWENTY- TO TWENTY-FOUR-YEAR-OLD POPULATION, 1968–1969

Sweden	18.8
France	18.6
Belgium	15.5
Yugoslavia	14.97
Denmark	14.9
Italy	13.6
United Kingdom	13.4
Netherlands	13.4
Finland	11.8
Norway	11.4
Germany	11.3
Switzerland	11.2
Greece	10.7[a]
Ireland	10.4[a]
Spain	10.4
Austria	10.0
Iceland	8.0[a]
Luxembourg	7.8
Portugal	6.7
Turkey	5.5
USA	43.3
USSR	33.00[b]
Canada	26.5
Japan	18.2

[a] 1967–1968.
[b] Estimate.
SOURCE: The *OECD Observer*, February 1972, 56.

the proportions of students in the total population twenty to twenty-four years of age (1967–1968). This method is "inflated" since it includes those under twenty (and over twenty-four) in university statistics but excludes them in population statistics. If a correction is made for this inflation, the proportions are substantially reduced, as is apparent from Table 3. These figures are obtained when only students of a given age group are compared to the population of the same age. Not only are the student ratios lower in each country, but the rank order of countries is thus changed. France, which was second in Europe in Table 2, is third in order after Sweden and Finland in Table 3; Finland has risen several places. In mass education countries, the USSR and Canada have had to exchange places. The leading position of the USA and Sweden has remained unchallenged, but in Table 3 Sweden's distance from Japan has increased.

The results of current methods of assessing the real proportion of the young generation engaged in higher education are unreliable. Though they provide some evidence of the scarcity of higher education facilities, the disparity of results between the different methods makes the determination of real scarcity very uncertain. In addition, for the purposes of comparison, such methods present fantastic problems of assigning proper weight to particular features of college attendance. As mentioned earlier, are freshmen and sophomores in American universities to be included? If so, what about US community college students or students in Soviet technicums? It is virtually impossible through these statistics to give a comparative picture on one side of the American college-educated cadre, reaching down into service occupations as far as airline clerks, nurses, and secretaries, and on the other of the apparently small European percentages, which often represent only those trained for upper-level professional and managerial occupations.

A more accurate method of estimating total higher-education attendance hinges on disregarding the passage from secondary to postsecondary education (Bereday, 1972b). Instead of being divided into primary, secondary, and postsecondary groups, the school population is separated into the universal compulsory group and the postcompulsory group. The transition between these two groups takes place in industrial countries between the ages of fourteen and sixteen. An analytical division of the school population at the watershed of sixteen years of age distinguishes the lower segment, in which almost the whole population attends, in which the curriculum embraces mostly basic general courses, and in which a spirit of tute-

Table 3
PROPORTION OF HIGHER EDUCATION STUDENTS IN POPULATION
OF AN AGE GROUP CORRESPONDING TO THE ACTUAL AGE
OF THE MAJORITY OF STUDENTS, 1968–1969

Country	Age groups	1968/69
Sweden	20–24	16.9[d]
Finland	19–24	14.0[c]
France	18–23	13.9
Belgium	18–23	13.8[c]
United Kingdom	18–22	13.5[c]
Yugoslavia	19–25	11.5[d]
Denmark	19–25	10.9
Ireland	18–22	10.0[c]
Italy	19–25	10.0
Norway	19–24	9.4[c]
Netherlands	18–24	9.0
Germany	20–25	9.0[d]
Austria[a]	19–24	8.3
Greece	18–24	7.65[d]
Spain	18–24	7.1[c]
Switzerland	20–25	7.1[d]
Luxembourg[b]	20–25	6.1
Portugal	18–24	5.7[d]
Turkey	18–23	4.4[d]
United States	18–23	35.0
Canada	18–23	28.0[d]
USSR	19–25	25.0[d]
Japan	18–22	14.1

[a] Austrian students only.
[b] 1965–1966.
[c] Estimate of enrollments.
[d] Estimate of age group.
SOURCE: OECD, 1971e.

lage over the young pupils prevails. In the second and older group, only part of the population attends, the curriculum is mostly professional or vocational, and a more adult attitude of semiindependent study prevails. Such a presentation is reflected in Figure 2.

This Figure reveals clearly a significant enrollment gap between the two groups of countries. In the mass education countries, the upper sector of the education system affects the lives of 35 to 45 percent of the corresponding population. There are European countries in which the leadership group is less than one-tenth the size of the total age group; but in the more advanced ones, 20 percent seems to be the rule. Sweden alone in Europe has attained almost 30 percent; since it is the only European country to have liberalized the upper reaches of its secondary education in the 1960s, this recent higher-education explosion is of particular significance.

The political and economic facts of life are substantially the same in all industrial countries of the world, whether in or outside Europe. But the levels of educational attainment of the managerial groups necessary to run these countries apparently are not the same. It is accepted that simply to live in them everyone needs eight years of basic general education. But for positions of leadership, a differential percentage of the age group, varying from 10 to 50 percent, has been needed and, therefore, admitted to further education. A philosophical question once more presents itself: Is it necessary, in order to mount a successful industrial system, to educate quite so many citizens quite so highly as the mass education countries have believed? If it is, Europe lags seriously behind.

Even more significantly, behind the front-rank European countries are those whose enrollment statistics still suggest the underdeveloped world. The relative attainment of the northern and southern European countries is different, while their forward momentum is similar. Consequently, the situation affords the low-achievement countries little hope of catching up. The rank order of growth among European countries changes, of course, from period to period but not enough to allow them to close their ranks. The average annual growth rates for 1962–1967 are shown in Table 4. Over a longer period the growth rates are homogeneous for Europe as a whole. Countries which lagged behind in growth in the first five years of the 1950–1965 period moved ahead in the second part. "No country can reasonably claim that the increase in its university enrollments during the last ten to fifteen years was 'out of proportion' compared to any other country" (OECD, 1969a, p. 5). This apparently heartening fact means, in sad reality, that the enrollment gap between the more advanced and the less advanced countries is

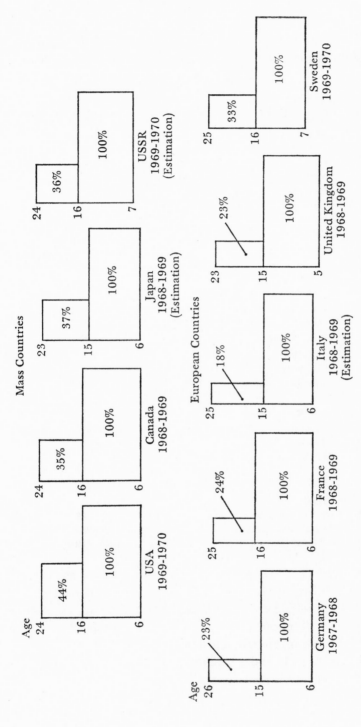

FIGURE 2. Comparison of postcompulsory attendance in mass higher education countries and European countries, by percentage of age group. For notes and sources see Figure 1 and note on page 21.

Table 4

AVERAGE ANNUAL RATE OF INCREASE IN HIGHER EDUCATION
ENROLLMENTS, 1962–1967

Sweden	16.4
Greece	15.7
Finland	13.8[a]
France	11.8
Spain	11.5[a]
Denmark	10.2
Turkey	10.1[a]
Italy	9.6
Belgium	9.1[a]
United Kingdom	8.7
Luxembourg	8.6
Portugal	8.5
Iceland	8.2
Ireland	8.0[a]
Netherlands	7.4[a]
Switzerland	6.4
Yugoslavia	5.7
Germany	3.5
Austria	2.9
USSR	10.8
Canada	13.8[a]
Japan	10.8
USA	8.7

[a] Estimation.

SOURCES: OECD, *Development of Higher Education 1950–67,
Statistical Survey.* Paris, 1970; for USSR, *Narodnoe Khoziaistvo
SSSR v 1969 Godu,* Izdatelstvo "Statistika," Moscow, 1970.

not being bridged. While all advance at more or less equal pace,
countries with relatively liberal admissions policies remain liberal,
and countries with restricted practices remain restrictive. Sweden
was the only European country to maintain a steady lead at the
top of the scale of growth, and among mass education countries,
Canada has recently had a similar spectacular record while Japan
may soon find itself in the same position.

Internal Links in Postcompulsory Education

The argument for lumping together all postcompulsory statistics is reinforced by correlations between the growth of secondary education and the subsequent growth of higher education, as apparent from a major recent report on this subject (OECD, 1971a, pp. 51, 53, 617). In most countries, neither demographic factors, nor economic wealth or growth, nor the propensity to innovations, nor student unrest, nor structural features, nor even admissions policies appears to be as closely correlated with higher education enrollments as are secondary numbers.

As regards population growth, only Switzerland seems to owe more than 50 percent of its enrollment growth to population increase. The figures for Denmark, the Netherlands, and Sweden were between 20 and 30 percent and for all other countries less than 20 percent. In a few countries population decline has even stimulated educational growth. A classic example was the expansion of Soviet education in the late 1950s when the generations born during the low–birth-rate wartime years reached senior secondary schools. The number of places available from previous years permitted accommodation of an increased proportion of that generation. In Europe an extreme example is found in Greece, where the high annual growth rate of enrollment (11 percent during 1955–1965) was accompanied by an important decrease in the age group (−2.9 percent in 1955 to −5.4 percent in 1965).

The countries most active in innovation between 1955 and 1965 were Yugoslavia and Britain, but with growth rates of 10.3 and 7.8, respectively, they were lagging fairly far behind countries such as Norway (14.5) or Greece (11.0), where during this period there were few innovations. In the late 1960s youth unrest was manifested forcefully in France, Italy, and Germany, countries with very different growth rates. From the structural point of view, countries with centralized administrative machinery, such as France and Sweden, have expanded very rapidly, but so have countries with a very decentralized administration, such as Canada and Yugoslavia. As regards admissions policies, the majority of the countries with the highest growth rates in different periods are those having no university entrance selection (Austria, France, Belgium). Several other countries with open admissions policies, however (Italy, Switzerland), are developing slowly, while other, somewhat selective countries, such as Norway and Sweden, have expanded enrollments as an increased rate.

Thus, we see that these correlations are rather unsatisfactory. But there is a steady and stable relationship between the output of the secondary schools and the intake of the university. The size of the terminal class in the former seems directly correlated with the changing growth rates of higher education enrollments. The secondary-school system is the real selective mechanism for higher education admissions. Secondary-school intake, the introduction of subjects preparatory to higher education, the dropout rate in secondary schools, and the host of factors affecting lower schools have a direct effect on higher education enrollments. Growing mass education movements in secondary education can therefore now be taken as sure signs of approaching mass higher education.

Innovations in secondary education, which thus assume a new relevance, have not been as extensive in Europe as in mass higher education countries. The goal in the most advanced countries has been to push up the compulsory secondary-school leaving-age to sixteen. So far not a single country in Europe has implemented this reform, and only Sweden, France, and England are within sight of doing so. Attempts to liberalize the secondary curriculum, such as the French *cycle d'orientation* or the German *Forderstufe,* have not been very effective. The sixth form continues to be regarded as a signal strength of the English senior secondary school, but recent research at Oxford has cast doubt on the superiority of specializing in two subjects as opposed to the European five. Only Sweden can really be said to have revolutionized its senior secondary education in the last twenty years, but even there it is not yet certain how well these measures have succeeded. Most Swedish students, instead of availing themselves of the new, more practical streams to higher education, opt for the traditional college-oriented curriculum. England has achieved significant reforms through its comprehensive schools, and there have also been some successes in Yugoslavia. But compared with the impact of such reforms as elective subjects in Japan, comprehensive programmes in Canada, and tougher science courses in the United States—or even the less successful polytechnization movement in USSR—European reform attempts in secondary schools must so far be judged inconclusive.

Innovations in secondary education have not swollen the ranks of secondary school students and therefore of university enrollments in Europe. Even with scarce statistical evidence, one may hazard the qualitative guess that innovations follow, rather than precede, increased enrollments. We are faced with a fact that might seem astonishing at first sight: with a given selection system, represented by set academic standards and examinations in each generation, an increasing proportion of the population succeeds in clearing each academic hurdle. The explosion of numbers has occurred and will continue *in spite of,* or at least without relation to, scholastic selection.

We shall have to face squarely the fallacy very current in Europe that increased enrollments must mean lowered scholastic quality. Such a view, which can easily be documented as a short-term phenomenon, is entirely unsubstantiated in the long term. Even without attacking this defensive attitude of academic elitism, Europe, Japan, and the USSR at least have witnessed an explosion of secondary and higher enrollments which occurred without any prior relaxation of the existing academic system and almost without disturbing it. The reasons, discovered by the North American countries, seem to lie in the historical development of literacy. The story of European university enrollment today is the sequel to the expansion of elementary education yesterday. Perhaps the time has come to lay down the axiom that *literacy, and hence the capacity for success in schools, is cumulative over the generations.* When literacy is limited, school enrollment can be limited. Once the circle of simple literacy schools is widened, the widening of the circles of higher schools must inevitably follow. The first generation illiterate produces a literate second generation, a third generation capable of traditional secondary education, and a fourth generation capable of higher education. Enough of today's intellectuals are the great-grandsons of ploughmen to make this simple historical truth self-evident.

"The demographic limits to a continuing and rapid quantitative growth are nowhere in sight," concludes an OECD report

(1969a, p. 55). Even in the United States, notwithstanding impressive regional figures in California or New York, the fact remains that as a national average less than half of the age group is attempting formal higher education. The European enrollment expansion demonstrates that there is no way to contain the educational ambitions of the population. It shows that the widening opportunities of one generation reproduce themselves as demand for education at a higher level in the next generation.

In traditional societies people were "born to their station." But in an industrial society each individual has in reality a dual role as both manager and managed. In some circumstances, the doorkeeper or the traffic policeman is managing people who are more highly educated than he is. Still, the higher the education, the more predominantly managerial the position. All postcompulsory education is designed to train for such positions. The ideal of mass education is that everyone should have access to higher education, both professional and purely cultural. But it is obvious that in practice it will be a long time before such an ideal can be fulfilled. Some terminal point will impose itself on the ambitions of mass education, and the limitation might very well be occupational. It seems reasonable to view the future of mass higher education in industrial countries as a 100 percent platform of compulsory general education on top of which will be erected a 25 to 75 percent structure of higher, more-or-less specialized preparation. Whether one-quarter or three-quarters of the age group is the more desirable figure will be the question around which arguments between egalitarians and elitists are now likely to rage.

THE BALANCE SHEET
OF
DEMOCRATIZATION

3

The modern school system is a giant sorter which separates people into status compartments. It can work either toward succession, in which son follows father at the same level, or toward mobility, in which the son's status is different and usually better. Any change in higher education in favor of the mass immediately affects the volume of hereditary education—that which perpetuates elitist succession. Equality of opportunity, the tool of reform and mobility, is a complex and confused concept. Efforts to democratize education are made or talked about everywhere, but lasting or significant results have been few. Education can be used for social ascent or social insurance. In mass higher education countries the working class rises to be middle class; the middle class, having ascended, is consolidating its position by using the schools to ensure that children do not fall below the social status of their parents. There is only a difference in degree between the mass education countries and the elitist countries. However massive the expansion of enrollments, sons (and daughters) of the favored have managed to hold on to an unchanging and substantial percentage of university openings. Neither social revolutions nor evolutionary programs of democratization have succeeded in any country in weakening the differential advantage of the sons of the social top quarter of the population, who continue to occupy more than half of all university places and thus enjoy much better life chances.

Methods of coping with this situation differ. European countries, selecting from elitist secondary schools for numerically narrow university entrance, are constantly concerned with who gets what. Many well meaning and some astute egalitarian programs, such as scholarships for the poor, have been tried, only to end in the chagrin of the planners because they wind up in the hands of the rich. Mass education countries, on the other hand, tend to play down the issue of democratization. They aim instead at widened secondary school output and increased university enrollment in the hope that the bigger the cake the less the bickering about the size of each slice. The mass higher education countries can hardly be said to have achieved significant success in dealing with disparities of educational opportunity, but their theoretical position on the issue holds out some promise.

The approach of the mass education countries to the class issue seems to recognize that there are two contending themes in education. The first, strong and most persistent, is class support. In all schools and at all times, people use education to maintain or establish themselves on the highest possible social plateau. When this effort is not controlled or counteracted, it becomes overwhelming and results in hereditary caste systems, even in education. Fortunately for those to whom such a system is repugnant the schools are also affected by a class-neutralization theme. Political beliefs, occupational necessities, and the self-generating ambitions of the masses diminish the power of class snobbery. Other counteracting influences are laws forbidding discrimination by religion, or color, compensatory remedial programs for students of impoverished cultural backgrounds, or insistence on educating everyone under a common roof to maximize contact between people from different social environments. Egalitarian wisdom applies as many of these safeguarding mechanisms as possible in the schools to keep in check the constantly emerging inequities. The result is not static equality but dynamic equalization, a *Gleichschaltung,* not a preventive, deterrent regime but an optimistic, upward, compensatory cultural movement. At issue is the narrowing social distance between different classes and the occupations supported or created by education. "It does not matter who gets what if all succeed according to their merit and if the positions reached are, after all, not so very far apart" (Bereday, 1968, p. 17). Even in the USA but certainly in Europe planners have yet to consider the implications of this proposition.

Elitism

In the old days poor children occasionally worked their way up the educational ladder sponsored by wealthy patrons or institutions. Adopted sons in Japan, favored serfs patronized by their Russian landowners, poor scholars in the early foundations of Eton or Winchester appeared in the educated class in almost every generation. But this mere trickle never obscured the fact that most opportunities for higher education went to the sons of aristocratic or economic elites.

Some schools recruited by birth. The *Ritterakademien* of Germany and Cadet Corps of Russia, for instance, were restricted to sons of the nobility. Even today, astonishingly enough, the Surovov and Nakhimov Military Schools in the Soviet Union are said to admit only the sons of the officers. More prevalent is the historic pattern favoring wealth. In the English private schools the increasingly wealthy bourgeoisie was able to merge with the older landed elite. Even the education of Chinese mandarins, because of its high cost, favored the sons or proteges of the rich. In England succession to high status through education was institutionalized as a channel for younger sons for whom families bound by primogeniture could not otherwise provide. In the United States, clauses favoring the admission of children of alumni have been deleted from the statutes of the Ivy League colleges only since the end of the Second World War and still remain the policy of many private schools.

The arrival of "equality of opportunity" has not basically changed the picture. It took only a few decades for egalitarians to realize that systems of intellectual selection still reward the sons of the favored classes. In technological societies, the educated are the ones who become well-to-do. There is therefore great pressure on schools to provide the key to higher income and status. But those at the top of society obviously have greater power to manage the system to their own advantage. Capacity for scholastic success is also related to class. Thus, because of intellectual as well as social factors, the sons of the well-to-do have no problem whatever in capturing a disproportionate number of openings in the schools. At the end of the Second World War hereditary succession in education was virtually undisturbed, with educated sons replacing their educated fathers in high-prestige social positions and jobs.

Many individuals and schools of thought, from Vilfredo Pareto to Jacques Barzun, find the connection between education and high social status beneficial. If one looks at cost alone, "it is preferable, although directly counter to educational justice, to recruit the general run of students in those social strata whose culture is nearest to the level of academic education, rather than to go and 'rescue' them from worker or peasant environment at the cost of a greater and necessarily more expensive pedagogical effort" (Grignon and Passeron, 1970, p. 66). Educational justice is at best an elusive concept. Inherited talent is still talent and ought to be encouraged because of the service it can render to its possessor and to others; its frequent appearance among the higher classes of society makes democratization difficult. People implicitly hostile to egalitarian policy demand that serious consideration be given to the liabilities of counterelitism. According to them, democratization, however noble and well meaning, exacts a heavy price. They argue that the cost of egalitarian measures is formidable, if only because competition from newcomers frustrates some career expectations of the upper classes. It also forces down the general cultural level of the highly placed, while increasing the tensions and insecurities of the social newcomers. The elitist view is that society is better off when the boat is not rocked and everyone can enjoy settled expectations. This view may or may not have merit, but since it is still firmly entrenched in many universities, thinking about democratization can only be enriched and refined by continuing to give it due weight.

The trend, however, is away from hereditary education toward some version of an open system. The mass education countries have created a new model, and Europe hovers uncertainly on the brink of adopting it. A parallel can be drawn with the way Americans handle their economic problems. Rather than seriously attempting to stop the rich from getting richer, they try to make the poor richer, in the belief that when everyone's standard of living is high in absolute terms, there is less concern with how rich any man is in comparison with any other. To avoid arguments about the justice of selection for higher education, efforts have been made to provide it for anyone who wants it and to compel or gently persuade those who do not want it to get it anyway.

In practice, in all countries, access narrows as the student grows older, and final enrollment among the elite is probably just as closely correlated with class in mass countries as it is in Europe. Certainly the proportion of sons of blue-collar workers in higher education (and, therefore, of those who are not the sons of such workers, whoever they may be) is not much greater in the USA than it is in Britain. The theory of mass education, moreover, is always haunted by the fear of overproduction of the highly educated. Sociologically, it is exciting for the egalitarians to envision policemen with law degrees and mechanics with Ph.D.s. But psychologically, so long as present patterns of prestige and rewards persist, it is not easy to persuade people who have spent many years in the hard study of law or advanced engineering to don with joy the policeman's uniform or the mechanic's overalls. Expansion of educational opportunity is more a felt than a reasoned need. It may mean some unemployment in the learned professions, and it is bound to lower the overall market value of high educational qualifications.

Several other factors, however, make the mass model distinct and promising. Compulsory schooling is lengthened, forcing a mass of people into preparation for higher education, regardless of their demand for it. The schools are coaxed to introduce increasingly elective curricula, allowing students to be more flexible and to develop better judgment regarding different career needs. The successful establishment of such patterns may mean that the prestige of mental and manual occupations will be increasingly equalized, thus creating greater harmony and cooperation between college graduates and noncollege-goers, the two social strata likely to emerge from a functional social system which assigns people to careers solely by level of education (Bereday, 1971b, pp. 111–122).

Evidence from the mass education countries shows that tensions associated with restricted admission, such as those Europe is experiencing, tend to disappear as access widens. The examination barricade which still surrounds the universities in the USSR and Japan sends shock waves down into the school systems which traumatize the middle class and discourage the working class. Few such tensions exist in the United States where, taking the country as a whole, the passage from high school to college is no more tempestuous than the progress from grade school to high school. In all the mass education countries tensions immediately appear wherever elitist selection survives. The Regents Examination in New York State creates conditions no different from those which exist wherever examinations bar access to universities. Competition for places in the prestigious Ivy League schools in the United States, in the politically powerful Tokyo University, or in the towering Moscow University with its metropolitan attractions is even fiercer than in Europe, where, as already noted, most of the selection and competition takes place in secondary schools. These universities and their offshoots combine excellent professional training with the power to confer superior social status. Elitist in character, they are pockets of struggle over admission, which reproduce in miniature the tensions existing on a national scale in elitist countries.

By opening admission, the mass education countries are more likely in the long run to escape the knotty question of how to apportion their university places. Open admission has come to mean, or will come to mean, that the highly educated class has an increased proportion of the population. It is already difficult to distinguish lower-level white-collar workers from skilled blue-collar workers on criteria of income, occupation, or even culture. In the mass education countries as a whole, the selection process is fairly smooth, because those who are rejected by one school, whether in New York or Moscow, find it relatively easy to be accepted by another. The more people are admitted, the larger and more heterogeneous is the resulting elite, and the more likely they are to introduce a flexible curriculum for the next generation.

Mechanics of Democratization

Doubling and trebling the university population means very little if the result is a leadership group which is still a tenth rather than a quarter or a half of the nation's relevant age group. In discussing their higher education problems Europeans speak of mass higher education, but such language merely confuses the issue; for with their relatively low enrollment rates, Europeans tend to use archaic approaches and dream of democratization, by counting workers' heads rather than grappling with new mass solutions. Their egalitarian efforts are courageous and admirable, but they are almost always doomed to failure.

Reports from all countries after twenty-five years of effort reveal that the advantage of the poor man's sons in higher education has not significantly improved. In France, one is "obliged to note the almost complete immobility of the social structure of the student population between 1961–62 and 1965–66" (Grignon and Passeron, 1970, p. 2). During that period the population of upper-class students decreased a mere 1 percent from 32.5 to 31.5. The proportion of farmers' children was equally stationary between 6.2 and 6.4 percent. The children of workers fared 50 percent better (6.4 to 9.4 percent). By the middle of the 1960s the bulk of places, 47.3 percent, still belonged to the middle class, with a grand total of nearly 80 percent in the hands of the privileged. In England, similar research reports for 1958–1959 state that 25 percent of students were working-class, a higher percentage than that in other European countries, such as Norway (20 percent), Belgium (14 percent), Netherlands (8 percent), and France and West Germany (5 percent). But the English proportion, too, remained remarkably stationary over the years. "Between 1928 and 1947, 8.9 percent of boys aged 18 from the non-manual classes went to university compared with 1.4 percent of manual working class boys, a ratio of 6.4:1; in 1960 the corresponding percentages were 16.8 and 2.6, a ratio of 6.5:1" (Perkin, 1969, p. 102). The picture is the same in Germany:

*In the Federal Republic of Germany about 50 percent of the popu-
lation are members of the working and farming classes. About 6
percent of university students come from this social group. The population has hardly changed within the last 15 years, i.e. the absolute
number has increased only in proportion to the total number of students. Even the introduction of a national stipend scheme for all
students from families whose income lies below a certain per capita
level—the so called "Honnef Model" scheme which, at present,
supports about 20 percent of all students—has not had a significant
effect in that regard (Boning and Roeloff, 1970, p. 59).*

The situation hardly varies from one European country to
another. Even Yugoslavia with its devotion to socialist purposes has
not been able to achieve any substantial alteration. There, in 1950–
1951, children of workmen and farmers held 30 percent of university places while children of civil servants, professionals, and shop-
keepers held 66 percent. Ten years later the proportions reported
were 33 and 63 respectively (Institute for Social Research, 1970,
p. 62).

This somewhat doleful account shows that most measures
taken by European countries to enlarge the representation of the
lower orders in higher education have not been successful, and most
were hardly innovations. Scholarships for the poor have existed in
several countries at least since World War I; though their volume
has increased, the very slight enlargement of working-class representation reveals that many scholarships are being captured by sons
of the middle classes. Several grants in England and the already
mentioned Honnef allowance in Germany were specifically designed
for family budgets which could not be balanced without the earnings foregone by their children while attending school. These, too,
had small results. A much more striking innovation of the post-war
era was the encouragement and financial and moral buttress sup-
plied to "lower-class higher education." The emergence of the whole
nonuniversity sector of higher education, best dramatized by the
British binary system, is one well-known example. The political out-
look as well as the social composition of the binary institutions, especially the Polytechnics, have turned them into militant spokesmen

in favor of mass education. Their impact on the social composition of the total student population, however, belongs to the future. As their status improves, they too will probably be captured by children of the middle classes.

The situation is not dissimilar in the mass higher education countries, though the ratios of worker's sons have improved. In the USSR, the leader in these percentages, the fifty years since the Revolution have rather brusquely introduced large numbers of new arrivals from the factory and even more from the village, but the hold of the sons of the intelligentsia old and new, though greatly weakened in politics, has not diminished markedly in academic affairs. Members of the rural and urban working class form 75 percent of the total population, but in the universities, according to Soviet figures for the late fifties, their sons were 30 to 40 percent of the total. Soviet sociologists have recently begun studying educational aspirations, and even in this inconclusive area 91 percent of children of specialists but only 74 percent of workers' children expressed a desire to enter university (Pennar, Bakalo, and Bereday, 1971, pp. 127, 129). In Japan, only since World War II have the sons of the samurai begun to relinquish their monopoly on university education to others, mostly the middle classes. Official figures for 1962 give 72 percent of students as being of higher social origin and 37 percent of lower, the reverse of their proportions in the population. Commenting on the comparative equity of Soviet and Japanese figures, Passin (1965, pp. 121–122) writes:

We can say that in the Soviet Union the population group that constitutes the upper 20 percent of the population contributes 50 percent of the university students or two and a half times its proportion in the population, while in Japan, the upper 34 percent contributes 73 percent of the university population, or slightly more than twice its proportionate weight in general population. From this point of view, there would appear to be more mobility in higher education in Japan than in the Soviet Union.

Japan and the USSR are new arrivals in mass higher education, but the social distribution of their students is similar to that in the United States. The USA with its vast opportunity pool and official good intentions still is not exempt from charges of discriminating against the disadvantaged. From among several available sources figures provided by Robert Havighurst (1971, pp. 271, 275) show that sons of the lower working class occupy 5 percent and sons of the upper working class 30 percent of university places, though they comprise 17 percent and 57 percent, respectively, of the total population.

All disadvantaged students are penalized by internal prestige patterns in American higher education, so that lower-class talent gets crowded into low-quality institutions (Hansen and Weisbrod, 1969, p. 114; OECD, 1970c and 1970d). These sources rightly deplore the frustrating waste of potentially good students whose ambitions are met by substandard education.

But anyone who has made prolonged visits to even the humblest community colleges in the USA ought to pause before denigrating the tremendous thrust and optimism and freshness of these institutions, largely compensating for their usually modest intellectual standards. The ascent of able lower-class students is also facilitated by large university graduate schools, which are much less socially and even intellectually restrictive than the undergraduate colleges at their own institutions. The steady emergence of highly successful professionals who begin in obscure colleges but become legitimized by prominent graduate schools demonstrates the important function of graduate education. When concerns about working-class representation are superseded by a concern for expanded opportunities for all those who are willing and able, there is an automatic increase in the egalitarian potentialities of the system.

In fact, the whole question of working-class representation is something of a red herring. When one encounters individual lower-class children to be educated, one is at once aware of the educational tragedy forced upon them, "the symbolic violence" of which Bourdieu and Passeron (1970), as well as Freire (1970) and Illich (1971), write so eloquently. The sterilization of human minds perpetrated in the name of knowledge by lifeless or calcified educational institutions is one of the most poignant dramas of the age of mass education. Also, when facing the force and freshness of working-class talents and ambitions, one is aware of the pain caused by the frustration of such thrusts when they are turned away by some arbitrary dicta of the often petty educational tyrannies. But these tragedies and frustrations have little to do with the argument that working-class sons should be represented in higher education exactly in proportion to the number of their fathers in the population. Such a doctrinaire position only postulates one more senseless rule for the milieu in which senseless rules are at last under attack. It implies that the working class is a homogeneous constant and has clearly distinguishable numbers in the population, which is nonsense. It implies that academic ability, however defined, is equally distributed in the population, which we know to be false. Most important, it ignores the effects of the ascent of families from one generation to another. Joliot *pere* is a worker. Joliot *fils* is a university student, and so is Joliot *petit-fils*. Joliot II is carried as the son of a worker in university statistics, but Joliot III appears as the son of a bourgeois. Yet, the history of the Joliot family is the history of democratization even if it is at the same time a history of *embourgeoisement*.

The central problem in technological societies, which are always starving for more talent, is not what proportion of university seats is reserved to working-class sons but how to make all talent, wherever it can be found, available in society's managerial positions. The mass higher education countries strive to ensure minimum frustration of talent flowing from the lower strata and minimum displacement of talent found in the upper levels. Their second priority is that talent which does get caught in the system of education does not then get turned off by insistence on obsolete, formalistic standards and rules. The beauty and worth of intellectual life lie in its freshness. When accumulated treasures of mankind are offered to young minds like stale vegetables, even an entire freshman class of working-class sons, as Soviet universities have found, will not improve the quality of education.

Mass higher education countries have not yet succeeded in solving the problem of lower-class frustrations by simply shifting emphasis from a stringent regulation of the flow of the educated to a less discriminatory upward promotion of many. But their work is not finished. There is a strong possibility that, given time, their ap-

proach will permit them to achieve a high degree of social harmony
in higher education.

Other Inequities in Higher Education

Class distinctions in higher education are the major factor of
inequality and as such dominate reformist concerns. But there are
other distinctions, some of which subtly reinforce the central social
divisions.

First, geographical inequities. Unequal geographical distribution of entrants is common in mass education countries. In the
American education system as a whole, overall regional disparities
are decreasing, since enrollments in high-attendance regions are
reaching the saturation point, while enrollments in low-attendance
regions are expanding at a steady rate. But in higher education,
regional differences have been, if anything, widening. The chances
of admission to Ivy League schools of students from the eastern sea-
board are always better than those of students from other regions,
in spite of assiduous efforts by these colleges to recruit according
to geographical quotas. The possibility of admission to the much
sought-after Tokyo University is greatly enhanced for graduates of
prominent Tokyo secondary schools. In the USSR, out-of-towners
cannot qualify for admission to Moscow University unless they have
secured a place in the dormitory or a room in the city. The only
limitation on students from Moscow is that they may not qualify
for a room in the dormitory. In Canada the best-known institutions
are located on the eastern and western seaboards and close to the
southern frontier, leaving young persons from central and northern
Canada at a disadvantage.

To these residential inequalities Europe is no exception. The
new universities in England are deliberately scattered regionally to
supplement the already existing network. This distribution reflects
awareness that British working-class youth are reluctant to leave
home and prefer to attend college locally. But in spite of this effort
the new British universities not only are overwhelmed by middle-
class representation but are also said to recruit nationally instead of
regionally. Reports which stress the geographical variation in Swedish university recruitment relate it to the lack of institutions in sev-

eral regions and to the student composition of the secondary schools, which also favor urban children (Englund, 1970, p. 14). In Germany the difference between the percentage of working-class children in the new university of Bochum (nearly 13 percent) and their percentage in older universities has been attributed to a belief "that children of lower income groups tend to go to the nearest university, or not to go at all if none is near" (Boning and Roeloffs, 1970, p. 58). In France the university population is predominantly urban and, as in most countries, tends to cluster in urban centers. The Paris region, with 2 percent of the population of France, houses 38 percent of all the country's students. In Italy and Austria regional disparities were "not appreciably altered" and were "as great in 1964–65 as ten years earlier" (OECD, 1970b, pp. 14–15). Only in Yugoslavia are the less developed regions reported to be providing proportionately more students, but the majority of such students are said to come from the larger urban units in such republics.

Scholarship schemes have been used widely to offset these patterns of rural disadvantage. The building of student hostels has also been approached imaginatively and extensively, such as those in England, Sweden, and Finland. Their operation has not been adequate, however, to offset the adverse rural-urban ratios. More significant have been efforts to fill the university map by creating new or upgrading existing provincial institutions. Trondheim and Tromso in Norway and Oulu in Finland are dramatic examples of bringing higher education to sparsely populated northern regions. In all countries under review the new universities have been created with regional needs in mind. But, once more, all these activities have been insufficient to redress the balance of access from remote areas. Statistically speaking, the picture is not dissimilar in mass education countries, but because they are mass-oriented and thus highly saturated with schools they create an impression of relatively even distribution.

Discrimination against women is our second category. The most successful recent democratizing trend has been the improvement in the ratio of women students. The record has been extremely varied from country to country and no meaningful distinction can be drawn between mass education countries and the European countries. All the former are coeducational at the primary and secondary levels, whereas a substantial number of European countries are not. In higher education, most countries are coeducational in theory, but even in those with high overall attendance of women, some faculties such as law, medicine, and engineering are virtually closed to them, while other specialties such as teaching have disproportionately high numbers of women. Among mass education countries, overall enrollment of women is highest in the USSR, nearly 50 percent, with the USA following at almost 40 percent. But among European countries Finland, Sweden, and France, surprisingly enough, exceed the latter percentage.

Japan, though it has registered substantial increases in certain sectors, is lower in the enrollment of women. In upper secondary schools the percentage of girls increased slightly in the years 1957–1967 and is now at 48 percent. Women exceeded men in general education and commercial courses and they increased their hold on the junior colleges from 62 to 82 percent in that decade. But in the universities, though they outnumber men in literature and education, their overall enrollment is now a mere 17 percent. Forty-eight percent of primary schoolteachers and 22 percent of secondary teachers were women in 1965. The official caution of 1918 "that the unlimited increase of female teachers would pose a problem to the raising of the 'sturdy and serious people,' " was revived in 1958 by the Central Council for Education (1969, pp. 40, 138). Japan does not rank in female enrollments with mass education countries because of old Oriental traditions which are slow to give way. It must be listed with those European countries which still register the lowest percentages of women in universities (Netherlands, Switzerland, Spain, Denmark, Austria) (OECD, 1971a).

Proportions of women students are also affected by an age shift. Primarily because of marriage, they discontinue at an early age.

In the majority of countries under consideration the peak of enrollment of women is reached at an age younger than that of men. The age of entry of women is in fact lower and they leave earlier than men partly because they choose courses of study shorter than men (especially in countries where non-university type higher education represents an important proportion of the total: Belgium,

Denmark, Netherlands, U.K.), partly because they abandon .in larger numbers their studies of usual duration (in the case of university studies) [OECD, 1971a].

Despite these limitations, the rate of female attendance has been increasing steadily and in many countries is an important factor in the growth of overall enrollments. Although around 1965 men had two to four times as good a chance to enter, we face a slow but steady feminization of higher education (OECD, 1971a, pp. 53, 58).

The improved position of women is a cultural phenomenon. The difference between mass higher education countries and Europe is that in the latter no special innovation measures are reported to have been taken to bring the improvement about. Europe is still not affected substantially by the Women's Liberation Movement or even greatly disturbed by echoes of the ancient pleas of the British suffragettes. In most countries the habit of going through higher education is slowly becoming the style for women as well as for men. But the finishing schools of England or Belgium are still considered satisfactory, and nonuniversity education is considered more appropriate than university training in many cases. Mass higher education countries make much more of a concerted effort. In the communist countries several formerly male occupations, such as medicine, have become largely female, and many women can be found on "heavy" jobs such as piloting and engineering. Among noncommunist countries, the USA has developed distinctive patterns. Here, going to college prior to marriage has become an accepted cultural phenomenon, and the already high male enrollment makes rapid rates of increase in female enrollment almost automatic. The process is even faster in Canada, probably because it began more recently—between 1955 and 1964 14 percent of the total increase of university students in the USA was due to the rise in female enrollments; in Canada the figure was 23 percent (OECD, 1971a, p. 53).

With regard to racial inequalities, the United States has been convulsed for a century by the "American dilemma" of not being able to provide an equitable education for blacks. American blacks and other minorities began the slow ascent after the Civil

War into crafts and skilled jobs, but hardly further. A breakthrough occurred at the end of World War II when litigation against the "separate but equal provision" clause forced southern law schools, unable to provide separate legal training, to integrate. Within a decade there were enough black lawyers to launch a frontal and victorious attack on school segregation. The black experience of ten years of integration has strengthened a new black separatism in lower schools. But in higher education, open programs for black students lacking formal academic qualifications are just being established, and departments of black studies, which furnish a new avenue of academic success as well as provide new pride and prestige for blacks, are mushrooming. The United States is also committed to continued efforts to assimilate and upgrade through education its many groups of immigrants.

Other mass education countries face similar problems. The aspirations of East European immigrants and of Indians and Eskimos in Canada are overshadowed but not rendered less real by the special visibility of the French Canadians. The Soviet Union has had to contend since its foundation with the many languages and educational aspirations of its hundred and twenty nationalities. Even in Japan, which is nationally homogeneous and where no recognition has been given in education to minorities such as the Chinese and Koreans, there has been some recent discussion about the untouchable *etas* and about removal of their educational limitations (De Vos and Wagatuma, 1966).

In Europe, on the other hand, racial inequalities hardly figure in discussion of innovations. Ancient rivalries and tensions between the Scots and the English in Scotland or between the Finns and Swedes in Finland have been latent. But areas of tension persist everywhere. The grievances of Greeks in Turkey, of the Welsh in Britain, or the Irish in Northern Ireland frequently find their way into the press. Even more urgent are the problems of Jamaicans and East Indians in England, immigrant Turks in Germany, and Algerians in France. The national aspirations of these various groups sometimes complicate the lower educational levels. The Wallons and the Flemish in Belgium, French and English in Quebec, tilt about for their respective rights in education. But these pressures have not yet reached European university gates. No claims for proportional representation seem to be made by ethnic groups. Whatever the role of lower schools, the universities simply assimilate the minorities.

The ancient issue of religious discrimination is not a burning one in Japan, but it is alive in Europe, North America, and the USSR. In the USA and Canada, church colleges rely partly on their own sources of income and try to get government support for the balance. By and large they refuse the government any control over their academic activities and thus protect the education of their coreligionists from state interference. Apart from a question of taxation without representation the conflict between church and state seems quiescent. Constitutional freedoms guarantee access of students of all faiths to state institutions. In the USSR periodic reports on persecution of the Jews or hostility toward the churches cannot obscure the fact that the government is forced to keep reconciling its intransigence toward religion with the de facto sponsorship of the religious press and seminaries. In Europe the major issues are whether the government has the right to keep religion out of state schools and whether it must support religious schools. Such concerns are seldom translated explicitly into an issue of discrimination in higher education. Yet the prestige as well as the ethnic character of most religious institutions, certainly of Catholic colleges in the USA, suggest that some inequality of opportunity is related to religion. In Europe one learns occasionally of Bavarian disputes with the Protestant North in Germany, the war in Northern Ireland, Protestant grievances in Spain, or the already mentioned Wallon-Flemish conflicts. But most church-state discussion centers around lower levels of education: the privileges of nursery schools in Italy or financial aid to religious school pupils in France. There is no suspicion of inequities at the university level.

Democratization and Equality

No modern society can hope to maintain an educational system which every year tells four out of five of its citizens that because of their allegedly inadequate brains or unfortunate geographical locations they are unfit for further education. No nation can maintain its health and stability when it inflicts upon four-fifths of the lower managerial, but nonetheless managerial, class some form of education and social rejection. Over the years this practice certainly drives large groups of people to alienation.

The major point of this discussion is that, whatever its pitfalls and merits, entry into the age of mass education—which occurs when at least one-quarter of the relevant age group is trained in higher education—is insufficiently considered in theory and seldom achieved in practice. The theory of mass higher education does not hold any place, let alone a central place, in efforts to democratize intake into European higher education, for instance. Instead, European school systems, typical of the majority, emphasize the fair sharing of existing opportunities more strongly than the absolute increase of opportunities. The rapid expansion of student bodies everywhere has simply heightened social-class sensitivities. It has alarmed the elitists and intensified the fears of the egalitarians; the latter are concerned that the new places will be used to further expand the relative advantage of the "haves" rather than be reserved on a priority basis for the "have nots." Worry about the "wrong" use of the added opportunities looms large in the minds of reformist policymakers who, as politicians, must be ready to accommodate egalitarian pressures. Over and over again efforts to reform educational systems, as exemplified by those in Europe, are thus directed toward giving access and even preference to the bright sons of the poor in order to hold steady or even to diminish the proportion of the bright sons of the rich. The policy of increasing intake enough to give everyone a share, the main characteristic of mass countries, is still remote in Europe and tends to be overshadowed by efforts to decide how large a piece of the existing opportunities each group should have.

To American observers, conditioned to a nearly unlimited expansion of higher education, it must seem odd that the august halls of European academies resound with disputes about who gets what share of access. But centuries of habit cannot be changed overnight. The notion that the educational system must act as a central sieve of talent was born as an egalitarian notion designed to substitute meritocracy for the decaying government by oligarchy. The realization that meritocracy, too, tends to become hereditary revealed the paradox of its historical appearance under the aegis of equality. The false equation of equality with equality of opportunity has sown lasting confusion, from which a great many European thinkers and, indeed, some American, Japanese, and Soviet thinkers have not been able to disentangle themselves. To them, justice and equality mean simply revamping and some renovating of the composition of the elite.

As a result of old elitist traditions and a *selective* rather than a *mass* conception of democratization, some absolute limitation of university enrollments may permanently prevail. The present shake up of higher education, many European people argue, must only be endured. The trick is to play for time. Egalitarian pressures will dissipate themselves as they have in the past, with only a little reshuffling of the upper class. The ferment of the newcomers can be "unbottled" by skimming off and absorbing the brightest of the working class. A new blend will emerge from the seemingly endless arguments, as the ambitions of the sons of the have-nots as well as the established expectations of the sons of the haves are adjusted.

Forecasters in mass education think this attitude unrealistic. Real democratization cannot be accomplished within an elite system. In the early history of the Soviet Union when sons of families with "undesirable backgrounds" were barred from universities, their proportion at the University of Moscow fell to some 30 percent. Even that was high. It was apparently still possible for many such undesirable sons to acquire worker status by getting a job for three years in production. When in 1936 Stalin removed the prohibition, the slogan "the sons are not responsible for the sins of the fathers" caused the proportion of the sons of the Soviet well-to-do in Moscow University to rise to some 50 percent again. This fact is one of many that establish the iron 3 to 1 handicap of the sons of the poor in their competition for university places. What we know about inheritance of ability, environmental influence of class on early verbal skills, and the general relation of status and educational motivation makes such a handicap unsurprising. Higher education has always been monopolized by the upper classes, and in order to compete at all the poor need greater ability rather than equal ability. An elitist system by definition means discrimination against them and probably a lot of social waste.

Expansion of numbers by itself, if not accompanied by conversion to the philosophy of mass education, does not resolve the dilemma. If expansion of numbers is slow, a problem looms, again, of whom to exclude at entrance. When Western countries embark on a policy of democratization they have to decide whether frustrating young sons of the poor by excluding them means higher social cost than dislodging the bright sons of the rich. Until now it has always been easier to exclude the poor, but with changing patterns of political power, the reverse may one day become true. Without fast increase of places, the class struggle surrounding university admissions is likely to be formidable.

But even if expansion is rapid the problem is not simply how to identify appropriate talent among the poor and how financially to smooth its progression up the educational ladder. Expanding the number of university places and, hopefully, of jobs for the university-educated does not guarantee that "new" men can be smoothly drawn into the educational stream along with men enjoying hereditary education. Channels of success in education have a tendency to clog up when facilities designed for the poor are grabbed by children of the rich. Partial successes only complicate the issue, because the beneficiaries of early programs change allegiance. Those who demanded access when they were poor are often most vociferous in demanding exclusive barriers the minute they achieve some professional or financial success.

These views are confirmed by current experience in industrial countries. Most sources are on the whole pessimistic about the potential of present innovations to reduce the adverse class distribution of incoming students. Everywhere children of the well-to-do, of the professional and managerial class, are not only present in the university population out of proportion to their numbers in the nation as a whole but fill up a large share of new places as soon as they are added. The significance of elite selection is many-sided, and more progress has been made in some areas than in others, but it is not unfair to characterize the reforms of higher education now in progress as helpless to break the hold of hereditary elitism. Mass education countries are ahead of Europe in the effort to modernize their structure because they have accepted or are in the process of accepting the principles of mass education.

Mass theory cannot be reconciled with the notion that academic ability and programs designed to suit it are fixed constants.

A flexible curriculum accessible to all at all levels and the possibility that the academic talents of all can be upgraded infinitely are its basic concepts. If nations cannot bring themselves to accept these propositions their people will continue to be channeled into socially superior and inferior specializations according to ability—that is, a mix of intellectual performance and the socioeconomic forces that shape it. The system will continue to be skewed in favor of the sons of the better-off classes. Their systems, expansion notwithstanding, will not evolve all the way to mass education.

But one must not forget the two sides of the existing social imbalance. The fact that more than 50 percent of places are pre-empted by sons of the elite also means that just under 50 percent of places in each generation do in fact go to sons of the less privileged. The system deliberately creams off the ablest of such people and, by keeping them in a permanent minority, assures their assimilation. It also leaves the remaining working-class people bereft of their natural leadership, safely docile to endure the life assigned to them by fate.

The only unanswered question is whether technological advances will permit the permanent confirmation of such social arrangements. As more men are converted by technical progress from blue-collar to white-collar jobs, and as the general rise of the standard of living lifts more people to the middle class, there will be more people just on the edge of an academic career, in a position to and increasingly likely to dispute the old selection criteria according to which only some among them are promoted to the superior social status that comes from intense specialization. In addition to the "me-too-ism" of this frustrated lower-middle class an educational structure committed to intellectual elitism has to convince the stupid to like and accept their place in the system. There is something repulsively counterhumanitarian in such a proposition. Mass education countries were forced to abandon it and others may soon be forced to do so. The apportionment of people to different responsibilities in society will have to rely not so much on selection for talent as on natural differences in commitment and perseverance.

FROM
SUBUNIVERSITY TO
ACADEMIC EQUALITY

4

Every major explosion of numbers in the history of higher education has brought forth new institutions described and describing themselves as mass academies. Some of these perished; others were in time converted into institutions of high status. The cycle is repeating itself at present. We have already seen how the pressure of numbers and the demands for just selection are constraining universities in industrial countries to take up internal reorganization. As the third major facet of the new situation, they must now also deal with the militancy of the mushrooming subuniversity institutions.

There is nothing strange in the appearance of nonuniversity institutions or in their subsequent aspirations to university status. The moment the narrowly selective secondary schools and the competitive examinations for higher education began to produce rejects, a potent market was created for training them in academic as well as in practical matters. These students began seriously to question the justice of being assigned to an inferior station. As the chorus of protests and the level of tensions rose, all industrial countries including those in Europe have been forced to cope with this new phenomenon.

Increasing awareness of international comparisons will further boost this rising tide of academic ambitions. Diplomates of the dental technicums of the Soviet Union will wonder why their American counterparts are holders of doctorates in dentistry. *Semmongakko* (technical school) graduates in Japan will demand college degrees like those now available from Colleges of Advanced Technology and even from Polytechnic schools in England. Funeral directors in Canada will stipulate two years of college study as prerequisites to their licence, just as New York State has done. The intersecting constellations of teacher-training, commercial, and technical schools, which are no longer secondary and not quite tertiary, will insist on being permitted to intersect also with the universities.

Structuring Higher Education Reform

At least three strategies suggest themselves for mass higher education countries confronted with this pressure. The first and most frequently adopted is to place the universities as the crown and exit gate of the entire educational system. All lesser institutions must thus be defined in relation to the universities and must be either part of the path leading to the universities or a constituent part of a university. For good or ill, in such a system the universities dominate higher education. This role is a result of a long and ambivalent historical process. On the one hand, universities, unlike other schools, were meant to be communities of scholars, protected with special immunities, devoted to serene contemplation and good discussion, pushing forward frontiers of knowledge, inspiring intellectual endeavor, and ennobling by moral example. On the other hand, like nonuniversity professional schools, they were forced to act as a filter for the upward flow of professional talent. The duty of professors to teach, test, and certify their students as a means of selecting their own successors became in time the duty to qualify candidates for other, more widely demanded professions. It was logical: since the universities were centers of the highest intellectual excellence, their approval and certification of attainment automatically became the highest proof of all professional excellence. All human skills, mental and manual, seem to have their own internal scales of attainment, and men who practice them now demand that their upper reaches be certified by the university.

In our time this logic has turned a little sour. The universities became victims of their own success. What could be done fairly easily when numbers were small without jeopardizing the essential role of the universities as "islands of reflection" could no longer be done so well in the age of mass education. Maintaining the universities at the top of the educational structure will probably cause them to abandon their contemplative functions. The victory of the certifying functions will turn them into vast testing grounds of professional achievement and will, at least at first, damage their role as general education academies. As certifiers, universities must act as stern judges of the myriad lesser institutions, rather than as their benign counselors. Confronted with large numbers of students, they must provide returns on invested time and money of specialized professional skills. These urgencies make contemplation difficult. Perhaps a reflective year or two could end the academic track as frosting on the professional cake. This layer of training would be easier to create if it were established away from large-scale professional universities in small-scale institutions, such as those advocated by Paul Goodman. Or several new universities of England and Germany, by deliberately electing to remain small, could provide a model of the traditional academic discourse between faculty and students and at the same time crown the postsecondary system. But most known "small" institutions eventually become large under pressure. Thus, under the first strategy, universities are likely to abandon altogether their contemplative, theory-prone existence.

The second strategy which university planners are exploring is to set up an equivalence system between two sets of regulatory institutions, university and nonuniversity. The universities would continue their certifying function in the traditional academic sector while surrendering it in newly arising fields to more specialized but equal institutions. The boldest expression of this strategy is the British binary system, in which about half of Britain's postsecondary students are channeled into nonuniversity colleges from which they emerge (as yet in small numbers) with university degrees awarded not by the universities but by a national certifying agency of university equivalence. Such a system is aided by the love-hate relationship with the universities that characterizes the vast array of subuniversity institutions already in existence and likely to keep appearing in increasing numbers. There is probably not one among them, be it a plumber's technicum in Leningrad or a *sogetsu* flower-arrangement school in Tokyo, that secretly does not aspire to elevated academic status. But memories of snubs in past contacts with the academic world and exaggerated apprehension of more to come cause many such institutions loudly to proclaim their "separate road" to salvation and to support a binary ideal. The *Polytechnische Hochschulen* in Germany and conservatories of music everywhere exemplify ancient and successful precedents for a binary system. These precedents were established, however, in an earlier era when the flow of students into both the universities and the nonuniversity institutions was miniscule.

In the mass age, it has taken very few years to reveal the poor long-term potential of the binary system. Political pronouncements of equality for nonuniversity institutions sound well in election speeches. But too often the slogan of "parity of esteem" turns out to be an unfulfillable hope if not a mere smokescreen, and as soon as this is discovered the binary frame of mind is over. Having realized that they are being cheated, nonuniversity institutions make a renewed bid for university status. Nobody ought to question the sincerity with which the faculties of nonuniversity institutions presently attempt, somewhat like some groups of blacks in America, to attain a separate identity. But in the long run neither university equivalence nor racial equality can be attained by "negritude." The slogan of separate identity, by allaying the fears of antiintegration forces, is merely a good first position from which renewed efforts at integration and true parity can be mounted.

The history of professional study of pedagogy illustrates this fact. Workers in teacher preparation in the United States, for instance, early realized that they must make a bid for separate institutional structures outside the universities if pedagogy was to establish a separate professional identity. Without such separation, the study of teaching would merely subexist within the universities, as do the chairs of this subject in Europe, still integrated in the faculties of philosophy. The USSR provides confirmation of this lesson:

its institutes of pedagogy, built separately from universities, have enjoyed multiple growth and specializations, while chairs of pedagogy in the universities remain as limited in scope as are those of Europe. What happened in the USA once the divorce was completed and teacher-training institutions became autonomous and visible was a tremendous secondary effort at reconciliation and bridge-building with academic departments. In a bid for academic quality, obtaining joint appointments, creating cooperative and joint interfaculty programs, and finally achieving full inclusion as separate faculties have been the substance of this remarriage.

Existing and intended binary systems must test themselves against this historical lesson. The strategy of parallel university and nonuniversity structures is attractive to those who are willing to surrender tertiary education to the masses but are unwilling to hand over the universities. At present, all industrial countries are seriously though perhaps wistfully experimenting with some form of binary solution, but this attempt is likely to be only temporary, helpful only as long as absorption by the universities is feared or the universities resist the academic ambitions of newcomers.

The third strategy makes the nonuniversities paramount; the universities are no longer on top, nor do they share power. In this solution they would be entirely set aside from the system. Since the certification function has put in jeopardy their ancient significance, the universities would benefit from being returned to medieval simplicity. The intellectuals of today are, after all, the descendants of the old-time scribes and modest monks. This strategy implies removing all career training and all degree- and diploma-granting functions from universities and vesting them in other bodies, such as the Higher Attestation Commission in the USSR or the National Council for Academic Awards in Britain. Freed from mundane concerns, the universities would be at liberty to engage in cultural, nondegree discourse, like that undertaken by the Danish Folk High School, or in basic research of a type being done at the Royal Society in England. If they were to continue to certify anyone, it would be only their own narrowly conceived faculty successors.

There are some signs that under pressure of numbers and insistent cries for reform, old-style university functions are moving into research institutes and nonuniversity systems. In the United States, with its usual multiple solutions, the models include a structural distinction between the many teaching universities and the few national universities oriented primarily to research and graduate training. They include also a vast system of nonuniversity institutes —governmental, such as the National Institutes of Health; nongovernmental but public, such as the National Science Foundation; and private, such as the Brookings Institution. In these intellectual life of an academic type goes on with little or no teaching function.

Internally, the universities have long practiced a distinction between teaching departments and research institutes, with the same faculty "wearing two hats" through its membership in both. There are many museums, libraries, and cultural institutes where the true collegial life of the old university is probably preserved. The dream of the "House of Intellect" has haunted many great academics besides Jacques Barzun, and universities can still be observed whose remote serenity suggests old monastic quadrangles. Castles, villas, and camps located in beautiful surroundings have become places of intellectual "retreat." A wealthy society could certainly afford the luxury of "islands of reflection" uncontaminated by the tensions of raucus status-seeking.

Whether the universities wish to return to seeking pure knowledge is another matter. The universities have tasted power, and though academics gathered in them come most alive when pursuing knowledge, even to these refined men the old adage applies that "power corrupts and absolute power corrupts absolutely." As more and more academic entrepreneurs are attracted to the universities, the older type of renaissance professor gets crowded out or relegated to secondary status. Had power been retained by the reflective men, the universities might have remained havens of pure knowledge, though perhaps they would not be very efficient as organizations. But the world being what it is, and modern universities being "where the action is," we cannot expect more than partial implementation of the third solution.

The first strategy of reform, which leaves universities at the top where they have always been while adding other schools below, is most likely to be pursued. It will provide a great variety of ter-

tiary institutions, large and small, at which academic excellence
can be preserved and emulated while the excesses of university
power can be effectively restrained.

The Subuniversity

Professional training of a mass of specialists *through* the universities will probably prevail. The universities will be placed at the
center of the postcompulsory system, but in order to avoid forfeiting
their traditional academic role—which as large-scale bodies they
cannot maintain—upgrading of some lesser and smaller institutions
to university status seems inevitable, so that the burden of regulatory
functions may be shared. This upgrading can be accomplished in
at least two ways: first, by promoting independent institutions to
full rank; second, by "articulation," by knitting minor institutions
as dependents into the existing university system.

Successful development of the subuniversity has been historically dependent on structural separateness. Here the distinction between a college and a faculty is useful. The image of a faculty
within a university suggests a dependent connected organization
whereas the college structure suggests independence. This dichotomy
comes into view not by juxtaposing Europe and the USA, the
USSR, and Japan but by grouping the USA, Canada, and England
on one side as representatives of the college system and continental
Europe, Japan, and the USSR on the other as representatives of
the faculty system. In the former three countries subuniversities of
all kinds have proliferated and grown. However, there are significant exceptions to this distinction. English colleges by being often
federated into universities have been, in fact, placed in a dependent
position despite autonomies they enjoy. They are not likely to secede
to become independent institutions. On the other hand, French faculties were granted by the Orientation Law of 1968 the right to
secede in order to form independent universities. The country of
greatest institutional proliferation, the United States, has a hybrid
structure, with English undergraduate colleges underpinning German graduate faculties. Japan's old faculty structure descends from
German precedents, although some current university nomenclature
and organization liken Japan to the hybrid United States. In view
of these confusing exceptions the college-faculty distinction merely

suggest rather than proves the notion that the rise of the subuniversities is associated with collegiate structure.

Linked with separate structure in subuniversity development is specialization. Before the eighteenth century, the pattern of higher education was uniform, resting entirely on medieval tradition. In England, Oxford and Cambridge (the only medieval foundations), in France, Paris, Toulouse, and Montpellier, in Spain, Salamanca and Valladolid, in Italy, Palma, Bologna, and Modena—these eleventh- and twelfth-century universities were based on a few established subjects. Thus colleges that grew into medieval universities were places of recognized general education. But industrialization made it necessary to move toward professional identification. Several European and American universities by necessity or design have adopted formalized or informal specialist concentration in order to obtain a better position in the pecking order. In the United States the University of Hawaii is noted for marine biology while Reed College, Oregon, excels in mathematics. In England the University of Reading is first in agriculture, while Sheffield excels in steel processing. Developing a strong point the way Konstanz in Germany has done in biology is an established device to gain rapid visibility.

Taking specialization of the subuniversities in its broadest sense, such as science, music, the arts, or economics and finance, all countries under review now have unisubject colleges as well as multisubject older universities. In all countries room has been provided for such as the Massachusetts Institute of Technology, the Himeji Technological Institute, and the École Polytechnique. Technical universities as well as conservatoria, academies of fine arts, and military academies are established national features of Germany or France or other countries. In the Soviet Union not only are the forty-odd universities overwhelmingly science-minded, they have been supplemented by more than two hundred specialized, unisubject, usually scientific institutes.

No unisubject institution predates modern times. Neither Salamanca, famous for medicine, nor Cracov, the alma mater of Copernicus, nor Peter Mogila's Academy in Kiev could be considered unisubject in its early conception, in spite of demonstrated interest in exact sciences. But by the nineteenth century specialized institutions abounded, and by the twentieth century the best of them occupied undisputed positions of excellence parallel with or exceeding that of the universities. Oklahoma Agricultural and Technical College is a vivid representative of the nineteenth-century type of foundation. Tokyo University of Education typifies twentieth-century creations.

Aspiring subuniversities intent on emerging with full status may follow two paths. The first and least usual is the transformation of unispeciality institutions not into unispeciality universities but into multispeciality schools. Karl Bigelow (1957) describes one of the most interesting examples of such transformation in the United States. Western State Normal School founded in Kalamazoo, Michigan, in 1903 for elementary school teacher training was transformed into Western State Teachers' College in 1927, into Western Michigan College of Education in 1941, into Western Michigan College in 1955, and into Western Michigan University in 1957. The acceleration of this transformation is worth noting. Such a general school does not often emerge from one specialized school; more frequently it comes about through federation of several unisubject institutions.

The second and more usual path is from subacademic unispeciality institution to full-status special university. This change is usually upward, for instance from Fukuoka Normal School to Fukuoka Teachers University, but the break up of a university into unisubject specializations also occurs. The separation of existing university components in France has already been mentioned. Another example is the decision of the Soviet Union and Soviet-influenced countries in recent years to detach faculties of medicine from the universities. The autonomous faculty within the university is a less extreme variant of this model. Teachers College, Columbia University, which has its own finances and a separate board of trustees, serves as illustration.

Upward subuniversity striving is propelled significantly not only by student pressures but by faculty tension. Only the oldest and most distinguished unisubject institutions now enjoy the prestige of universities. The world of higher education faculties, therefore, contains its own second-class citizens. Universities and quasi-university institutions stand on one side, steeped in the scholastic tradition of old and totally selective, if not frankly elitist, convictions and practice. Below that clear-cut level, there is a hodgepodge of institutions created in response to various needs and ambitions connected mostly with advances in crafts and technology. There is no common label for these grass-roots organizations, though some understanding of their history can be gained from studying nineteenth-century American land grant colleges. One could view the old universities as a rocky shore jutting out of the sea and the second-level institutions as waves bubbling below. In our time the crest of the highest waves is beginning to top the rocks and as they equal the height of the shore, they themselves begin to calcify.

The pressure of nonuniversity faculties to acquire recognition through university status is a basic part of the story of higher education today. In this process, the old clashes with the new. The ascent of new institutions tends to reduce the level of the old, bringing about a common denominator. And the new creations try to prove their status by denying the prestige of the old. It would be interesting to study the psychology of the vocalists in the two belts of higher education. We see on one side sympathy with the rising ambitions of the populace toward higher education and delight that more human beings will be exposed to high-level knowledge and that increasing demands for depth made by the industrial system can be accommodated. On the other hand, we face fears that the surge of the masses will deprive the old places of their lofty, rarefied position and that tensions between first-rate minds and those that have been made to feel they are second-rate will destroy the academy.

Faculties of nonuniversity institutions suffer acutely from inferiority feelings which periodic declarations about "parity of esteem" and attempts to bring about equivalence of their schools do little to alleviate. By their mandate and position, such faculties are aware of the aspirations and needs of nonuniversity students and frequently champion their cause. But by inclination the same faculties look up to the universities and tend to assimilate an elitist position. A passage from the Burgess and Pratt study (1968, p. 39) of the British nonuniversity system illustrates how these feelings come about and why elitism perpetuates itself.

[The] National Council for Technological Awards made no specific requirements for qualifications [for college teachers]. Indus-

trial and other experience was considered as valuable as academic qualifications, even at the level of "leaders of each branch study." This gave many people in industry the opportunity to teach in technical colleges, and gave the college the benefit of teaching staff with practical experience in their subjects. But the high standard set by the NCTA did mean that academically highly qualified staff were often more likely to get jobs in the colleges. In the CATs [Colleges of Advanced Technology] in particular, with improved salary and promotion prospects, an increasing number of staff had first and higher degrees and came from universities.

The chain of events is familiar. Efforts to maintain high standards, of which the universities are the best measure, result, even in practical-type colleges, in preference for university-trained men. Such men tend to press for conversion of their institutions to university status and university practices. A classic case comes from the United States. Two decades ago a young professor in New York was impressed by the demand for college education of a mass, local type, a demand which was soon to give rise to the community college movement. In a pioneering gesture he established such a college across the Hudson River in New Jersey, offering to all neighborhood high school graduates a variety of both academic and practical courses. A few years ago the funder resigned from the presidency of what had by then become a university. Rumor said that his departure followed pressure from his faculty, which wished to upgrade entrance requirements in order to become more selective. It took a mere decade in this fortunately isolated case for a mass institution to acquire elitist ambitions.

While we have to contend with academic snobbery on all sides, pretentiousness in some universities, and intellectual charlatanism is some subuniversities, the process of forming new university faculties goes on. The newest zone of aspiring institutions and faculties ranges from the polytechnics in England, junior colleges in the USA, and the technicums in the USSR to new universities, such as Aachen in Germany and Tokyo University of Art, which grew from humble technical schools.

A minor but interesting element in subuniversity ascent is exciting architecture. Through quality construction, the public can do miracles to enhance the appearance and public image of subuniversity institutions. In the United States, even in state-run universities, wealthy patrons anxious to see their names carved in stone are easily persuaded to endow new buildings. In the Soviet Union and Japan, where such finance comes from the state, it is equally easy to appeal to the national pride of the dispensing officials. The results can be seen in the University of Moscow complex on Vorobyi Hill and the Hongo Campus of the University of Tokyo. In Germany it has been estimated that the cost of providing a university plant equals no more than five years' ongoing expenses. This low cost has begun to produce pioneering campus designs with a central "forum" and buildings spread out according to a structural principle of "close interlacing of disciplines," as exemplified by Bochum and Konstanz universities (Boning and Roeloff, 1970, p. 127). In England recurrent grants for educational operation are separated from capital investment grants. The latter permitted some extremely imaginative campuses and buildings to be constructed, some in the old but especially in the new universities, aiming at the principle of integrated pedestrian campuses that would ensure long-hour residential activity. "The contrast between the bright lights and humming activity of the New University campuses by night and the dimness and deadness of many of the civic universities is striking testimony to the innovation this round the clock approach has already achieved" (Perkin, 1969, p. 89). From the East-West Center in Honolulu, a masterpiece of Edward Durell Stone, to the Institute of Technology in Othanieni, Finland, a creation of Alvar Alto, from the building of the National Institute for Educational Research in Madrid to the campus of the University of America in Bogota, vistas of untold beauty are being provided by college campuses. Wherever an integrated, well-designed campus replaces a Redbrick schoolhouse, a heightened academic consciousness is the instant repayment. A substantial upgrading of lesser-ranking institutions can be accomplished if specially earmarked resources for construction are imaginatively employed.

Articulation: Connected and Discontinuous Systems

The theme of ascent through specialization has to be supplemented by a second theme: the search for dependent union instead.

As an example, while American teachers' colleges rose to independent status and came to join universities as full faculties or even to turn themselves into full universities, teacher-training colleges in Britain had to content themselves with status within the institutes of education presided over by the universities. The latter path to academic recognition is less likely to be permanent because once within the university structure the newcomer colleges often experience heightened appetite for more prestigious positions. But at present vast systems of interdependent tiers of institutions have been built and are being advocated as a viable form of organization.

The connected structure of higher education can be subdivided roughly into three tiers. In the United States such tiers are called junior colleges, colleges, and universities; in Yugoslavia, a three-level system. More generally, they could be called nondegree, first-degree, and graduate-degree institutions. In different countries the ladder composed of these different parts is variously put together. Broadly speaking, it is the mass education countries that have achieved three-tier organization. In the United States the California system is the most complete example, with two-year colleges feeding into four-year colleges feeding in turn into university graduate schools. Most states, though in a more disjointed fashion, approach this type of graduated organization.

In Europe, though more loosely than in the United States, such organization exists inside the universities in the form of short diploma courses, regular degree courses, and long work on graduate degrees. But only in the United States, in the USSR and related countries such as Yugoslavia, and in Japan is the three-tier structure used as a grading scheme between as well as within institutions. This pattern of organization is so diffuse that it often looks like no pattern. An appropriate metaphor would be a cake with succeeding layers having different ingredients. Perhaps because the pattern grew spontaneously and indistinctly it has survived and is spreading. Whenever it exists it inhibits the ascent of subuniversities by tying them as dependent subunits into more eminent structures.

In the United States and countries of similar tradition, integrated colleges exist side by side with those intent on becoming independent universities. In the Soviet Union and Japan, because of greater similarity to Europe, the structure is less viable. In the USSR the technicums, at least in their long courses, are officially connected with the universities within the framework of ministries of higher education. Less clear is the place at the top of the structure of the *aspirantura* (graduate study) level. Training for the degree of *kandidat nauk* and often also later work on Soviet doctorates can take place within a faculty of the university but it can equally well be farmed out to another research institution, such as the Academy of Sciences. Only the fact that all such degrees are granted directly by the Ministry of Higher Education integrates the structure. In Japan the growing junior college movement and the revival of the technical *Semmon-gakko* has given the lowest level new importance. But the top layer, that of training for doctorates, is locked into the universities, and there are administrative peculiarities—such as the custom of permitting the submission of the thesis by invitation only, largely to protect the seniority of graduate students—that are almost feudal in character.

The various institutional levels are less clearly articulated in Japan and the USSR than in the USA. The structure is not clearly threefold but is at least multiple. Contrasts with Europe are difficult to make, but we can say that the pattern there is even less varied. In no country is the overall structure of higher education sufficiently developed to be threefold. University education consists usually of one unified degree track. The second track of education is just being created now that the nonuniversity colleges feel sufficiently strong to aspire to academic status. While the levels in mass higher education systems tend to be connected to each other, European subuniversities tend to remain disconnected. Lower-level institutions outside universities or short diploma courses within universities are present in France, Italy, and elsewhere, but many of them do not lead to anything at a next higher level. Their terminal character makes them marginal to the mainstream of university life. In quite a similar fashion, graduate training has not been institutionalized into the culmination of a whole study track as it has in the USA and, to some extent, in the USSR.

The patterns of innovation in higher education structure all seem to point in the same direction. Mass education countries are adding more introductory-level institutions than are the European countries, with the exception of England. Because such additions are made in a market fairly well saturated by second- and third-level institutions they tend to *stay* introductory for a long time and function for their original purpose. Direct creations at the second and third levels also tend to function at the assigned level.

In Europe there is an underprovision of facilities at all levels, and therefore new additions as well as old institutions tend to move upward quickly under pressure of demand. New low-level colleges are created or old ones streamlined but they tend to evolve rapidly in the direction of universities in the same way that prewar institutions founded in the USA have evolved. Old universities are pushed to reform and modernize themselves from within to embrace the specialized purposes imposed by the market.

The whole field of higher education is erupting like fireworks on a carnival night, but synchronization is poor. Old institutions tend to draw the new reformist universities into their conservative, established orbits. Pushed by society to become interdisciplinary, the newcomers tend to revert instead to a unisubject or subject-defined direction under pressure from the universities. Where higher education is being moved at all toward a polyversity or a unitary connected system, it reacts by erecting barriers within institutions, making interchangeability of students difficult—"the question of differentiation within" its walls (OECD, 1970b). The whole question of interinstitutional tranfer, an easy upward flow of students, looms large in relation to the build-up of junior colleges in the United States, but elsewhere, though considered and planned for, it has yet to be seriously faced. Mass higher education, though apparently bewilderingly diversified, means an orderly pattern of interconnected institutions through which a student can make a steady and continuous ascent.

The best argument for hooking ascending institutions into an established system is that past experience suggests they will be able in this way to secure the patronage of old universities. As independent, upward-bound colleges they are likely to incur the enmity of these universities, an almost irreversible obstacle to their progress. One is always tempted to hope that brilliant and astute central administration can with one great sweep set right what is wrong in education and that centralized power could by fiat order equivalence between all forms of postcompulsory education. Imaginative public dramatization of the issues and mobilization of impressive financing do boost into action government policymakers; but even brilliant reform proposals have been rolled back by an unwilling society. Few miracles are possible even for so strongly centralized governments as those of the USSR, Japan, and France. Successful paternalism notwithstanding, mass academies are wisest to look toward a grass roots movement and the support not of governments but of universities. Precedents for soliciting university interest have been established in many countries with the creation of new universities. An outstanding example of good linkage is Keele University in Britain, created with the initiative of Oxford and Manchester. Without university support, or at least acquiescence, planning for any section of higher education is not likely to become effective.

In all countries, academic planning is customarily entrusted to universities. Historically, most institutions, being independently incorporated, have depended on private endowment and developed planning in response to available finances. State systems continue to observe this endowment pattern in the rule that planning is generated by and not imposed on the universities. In England the University Grants Committee and other agencies concerned receive plans from the universities and simply adjudicate their conflicting interests. Even in new universities which are totally conceived and financed by the government the original planning comes from special committees composed of local citizens and friendly academies. Most other European countries also observe this rule, although in some, Germany and France, for instance, planning may be done by offices at the ministerial level, in consultation with the universities. The rule is certainly observed in the United States and Canada, where all universities, state and private, are expected to generate development plans. Even in the strongly centralized systems of Japan and the USSR planning blueprints acted upon by the respective ministries originate within the universities.

Government planning, in view of this ancient rule, is not likely to be significantly dramatic. The roster of efforts to plan for universities is small. In the United States proposals are being made to establish a National Foundation for Higher Education, and at the state level a majority of states have coordinating planning bodies. In Japan a master plan prepared in 1970 envisages the creation of the National Council for Planning Higher Education to supplement the existing Central Council for Education. In the USSR, the original home of serious planning, a Central Planning Commission (Gosplan) coordinates with the appropriate ministries the educational efforts of the country. Three separate commissions, the U 68 most famous among them, plan Swedish education. In Germany the Educational Council, the *Wissenschaftsrat*, has attempted for over a decade to coordinate the efforts of the *Länder*. From Norway to Turkey planning units attached to central administrative bodies, as well as special commissions, attempt to regulate the flow of innovations. Not only are these efforts few but their effectiveness belongs to the future. As stated by an OECD report on Britain (1970c, p. 9):

> *It is, indeed, doubtful how far the British planning agencies, which have relatively well-developed quantitative techniques, are yet willing to tackle even such topics as easier transfer between differentiated institutions, accumulated credits and qualifications, easier movement between work and education, and changes in the design and assessment of the curriculum. They seem even less willing to consider other qualitative issues as the proper domain of central planning and have doubts whether suitable techniques for planning them are available in the British context.*

Some similar characterization could be made of government planning machinery in most countries. The best we can hope for is that governments will through their actions gently coax the universities into a less reluctant position.

Prestige Patterns

One suspects that universities resist not only emergence of "upstart" equivalent universities but also a connected dependent system with themselves as the apex, preferring some form of monopoly instead, in an attempt to ward off, delay, and deflect the onslaught of the subuniversities. But if the experience of the countries of mass higher education is any guide, a balance of power within an integrated system of postcompulsory institutions of university type can be maintained. This balance is accomplished in practice (though this must be said somewhat cynically) by the prestige patterns that inevitably develop within educational systems. Instead of having graduate universities, undergraduate colleges, and junior colleges, or instead of building parallel systems of binary university and non-university institutions, one can simply opt for a system of legally equivalent postcompulsory institutions, whose formal gradation is replaced by a de facto but less visible prestige differentiation.

Prestige patterns are essentially damaging. High-status institutions are known to confer an occupational advantage and social prestige. Sometimes such advantages are derived from justice—that is, these institutions inevitably attract the accumulated talent and resources which produce excellent graduates. But just as often these advantages are a product of snobbery and unjustifiable prejudices. Just or not, such prestige patterns not only make occupational chances unequal but are harmful psychologically. By discriminating in admissions policies on social or intellectual grounds, or both, they visit rejection on many worthy people whose only crime has been an excess of aspirations.

These reprehensible effects of prestige differences are, however, somewhat offset by their potential to adjust demands for high specialization and particular excellence on one side with a broad egalitarian approach on the other. At worst, good institutions and those others not so competent are for general consumption disguised under common university nomenclature while supplying those "in the know" with means of discreet internal differentiation. At best, lesser institutions anxious for rewards of high prestige are induced to make concentrated bids for excellence in particular fields, such as bilingual training at the International Christian University in Tokyo or specialization in brewing at Birmingham.

In mass education countries prestige patterns tend to be less accentuated than in more traditional systems, but they are actually relied on to preserve desirable features of the old selectivity within mass intake. The USA structure, with a handful of prestigeful colleges at the top, better state universities in the middle, and others following them, is a way to reconcile the necessity for both high-powered academic milieus and low-key, open educational forums. High-prestige universities specialize in research, in training graduate students, in attracting the most brilliant or ambitious undergraduates. They act as model-setters, inducing competition between uni-

versities and providing for advancement of able undergraduates of lesser colleges in search of good doctoral training. There is a constant feedback. These graduate students subsequently percolate down into the system as faculty. The government and many foundations act deliberately to offset too great a prestige gap by distributing grants to encourage growth below the top level. Thus, tensions between the different social worlds within American higher education are deliberately converted into upward striving.

Similar pyramids of prestige exist in other mass education countries, but their workings are much less harmonious. The situation in the USSR and Japan, while appearing to be similar to that of European countries, is actually worse. European countries enter students from a restricted secondary-graduation channel through a restricted university entrance gate; the passage is relatively smooth. Japan and the USSR bottleneck a wide secondary-graduation channel with a narrow university entrance. The resulting rate of attrition is awesome. On the day admissions are posted, crowds stand in the university halls of Tokyo or Kyoto, and the silent shock of those rejected pervades the atmosphere. The old imperial universities of Japan act less as sieves to catch talent from below and more as monopolistic courts into which the chosen few are admitted and then sent out toward chosen jobs. Soviet universities follow a similar pattern. Whereas the ratio of those applying to those accepted is one to four for Soviet Union as a whole, ratios for the universities of Moscow and Leningrad may be as high as one to twenty-five. Recent data are not available to check how increased are Harvard or Moscow graduates' chances of landing the best jobs and enjoying the greatest social prestige. (Among more abundant reports for England, see Bereday, 1947.) Data for Tokyo University and Japanese universities in general suggest that "elite positions in Japanese society have been largely dominated by the graduates of elite universities—Tokyo Imperial, Kyoto Imperial, and Tokyo Commercial Universities (and to a lesser extent the other former imperial universities)" (Passin, 1965, p. 127). With time, given the rising status of other universities, Tokyo and Moscow will "articulate" more within the structure, but at present they are veritable bastions of monopolistic privilege. Little has been done by any means, let alone by measures as drastic as the division of the University of Paris into thirteen universities, to deprive them of their positions of leadership at the top of the system. Canada should be studied as a model of a fairly equalized university prestige pattern. But the rivalry of French and English universities in Quebec and the delicate position of McGill as a Protestant, English-speaking university supported by the Catholic, French-speaking Quebec government greatly becloud the issue.

Prestige patterns in Europe are destined to be scrutinized, and serious attempts have already been made to reduce their internal disparities. These efforts are especially important in England and France, where Oxbridge and Redbrick rivalries and the dominance of Paris over other French schools have made the admissions area definitely sensitive. In Germany, Holland, and Italy there was always relative equity between the universities, though fierce inequality between universities and nonuniversities. It is primarily in mass higher education countries and in England and France that previous attempts at abolishing social-class disparities between theoretically equivalent institutions have had to be made.

Britain is the leading innovator in this area and with reason, since more than half of her best jobs are known to be restricted to alumni of Oxford and Cambridge. Since the Second World War the number of students at these universities has substantially expanded, lessening somewhat their exclusiveness. Entrance requirements in Latin, which favored the chances of alumni of private schools over those from national education, have been abolished. After initial reluctance Oxbridge joined the central body controlling the flow of candidates to the universities. The central committee assigns candidates according to their stated preference but tries to balance social and talent distribution. Today Sussex, favored geographically and socially, has nearly as many applicants as Oxford. The numbers of maintained (state-supported) students at Oxbridge have tripled since World War II. This increase brought within the precincts of the universities a considerable number of grammar school graduates. The social tone of Oxbridge has not changed appreciably, owing to the considerable assimilating power of these universities—Britain has long and successfully practiced the art of blending the elite from among old and new social groups. But at least serious efforts were made to permit reshuffling; the broadening of the social intake of Oxbridge was the first step in this direction.

Circumstances have also favored the upgrading of Redbrick. Since the war they have been given a substantial financial and man-power boost. Prewar Redbrick universities were located in large in-dustrial centers, catered to commercial and municipal interests, and reflected generally middle-class interests in their regions. This focus hurt their social reputation in the eyes of the elitist academic com-munity. But the creation of new universities in small historic towns, more on the patterns of Oxbridge, with interesting architectural de-signs and experimental programs, helped to lift the public image of the older Redbrick. Furthermore, in attempting to build up the nonuniversity system of higher education to implement its binary formula, the British government effectively caused the upgrading of all universities. Now, the cleavages of Oxbridge versus Redbrick are lessening, drawing them together in the common cause of op-posing the nonuniversities.

The creation of the Open University, the first such in Eu-rope, promises to take university education into the homes of the poor. Education through media was hitherto practiced outside Ja-pan only in schools at lower levels, where it serves purposes of de-mocratization in Italy, Australia, and Colombia. The majority of registrations for the first year of British television university courses is reported to have come from teachers. But nonteacher registrants, including housewives, represent a beginning that should not be deni-grated. One must also watch the valiant, though so far vainglorious, battle of the British authorities to convince the public that nonuni-versity courses and professional diplomas are as good as university courses and degrees.

Similar efforts to diminish the interuniversity pecking order are being made in France to lessen the collosal domination of the University of Paris. As mentioned earlier, the Orientation Law of 1968 permitted secession of faculties. The host of new Universities of Paris then established may lessen the central image of Paris as a whole and of the Sorbonne in particular. But the law has done nothing to limit the power of the *Grandes Ecoles* to confer the high-est levels of university prestige in France. Some measures, such as the creation of the new degree of doctorate of the third cycle, can be interpreted as faint attempts to undermine the prestige stranglehold of the older, superior qualification, the "aggregation," through which most graduates of the *Grandes Ecoles* qualify.

The mass higher education countries have not concentrated on closing the prestige gap between the universities from above. Rather they strengthen the competing institutions below. In the United States public and private funds frequently go deliberately to new or remote institutions. Admissions quotas of all Soviet universities are regulated by the government. At Moscow and Leningrad, the two most prominent Soviet Universities, pressure for admission is incidentally limited, as already mentioned, by the available residential facilities. In Japan, although the supremacy of Tokyo has not been significantly challenged through government policies, the high social value given to private colleges, such as the Peer's School (*Gakshuin*), Keyo, Waseda, and ICU, does something to prevent Tokyo's dominance from attaining runaway proportions.

Attempts to reduce the disparity of prestige between the best universities and their lesser brethren are a proper and natural result of the "neutralizing" activities of policymakers. The emergence of a vast array of academic institutions small enough to ensure collegial intimacy and capable of offering good postcompulsory training may disorient the market sufficiently to permit paring down the extremes of social stratification. The prospect for mass academies is simply that "external" formal and legal disparities between different postcompulsory institutions might be dispensed with in favor of a legally equalized system. Everybody knows the sociologically obvious— though not altogether happy—fact, which may be offered as a consolation to the opponents of equalization, that a homogenized higher education system would still contain internal, perhaps somewhat less stringent but nonetheless functionally effective, prestige differentiation.

The message for elitist countries from mass education countries is that diversity within unity can easily replace the present legalized pecking order. No country, of course, is committed completely to the system of universal postcompulsory academies. But insofar as the United States and others have been driven in this direction, one can see from the history of their secondary education how little loss of prestige and how much gain in striving for status as well as excellence occurred when those schools which elsewhere are still obscure senior elementary or trade schools have been digni- fied by conversion to high schools. Today few would insist that a mass high school, though different from them, is inferior to grammar school or *lycee*. By analogy the future may provide little reason in the name of good health in higher education in, say, the state of Ohio, to "put down" places such as Slippery Rock State Teachers' College by barring their way into the community of universities. A much less extreme prestige pattern has come into being between the teachers colleges which grew into Kent State or Bowling Green University and the old University of Ohio at Athens. Upward equal- ization is a matter of dignity, of healthy competition, and finally, in the world of knowledge, of sheer human decency. Comparative evi- dence suggests that we gain nothing from applying to the world of higher education a repressive philosophy.

FACULTY REFORM
AND
STUDENT POWER

5

"A university is not a school in which the teachers impose their dogmatic views and rules of conduct upon the pupils but a community of scholars, senior and junior, devoted to the common and mutually illuminating pursuit of learning. Such a community is not, on the one side, an oligarchy, in which the qualified few make all the decisions and the unqualified many must blindly obey; nor is it, on the other, an ochlocracy, in which the numerical majority of students has the democratic right to impose its will on the minority of academic staff. It is a professional community of unequals, in the sense that the older and, if not wiser, at least more experienced, devotees of learning have the right and the duty to lead, influence and explain their expertise and ways of thought to the younger and less experienced members" (Perkin, 1969).

The balance of judgment expressed in this elegant statement describes the university of yesterday, or so we would like to think. We would also like to think that the professional community concept expressed may be the basis of tomorrow's university structure. But only with an effort can this idea be accepted as the essence of academic governance today. So much agitation has passed through the body of higher education that society's faith in the fit between the ideal of the university and the reality of internal structure has been undermined.

One curious feature emerging from this passage deserves special notice. It speaks of the community of senior and junior members, the teachers and the students, but it actually refers to senior teachers and students alone. No mention is made of the middle-range people, the junior teachers, that vast but not sufficiently visible group who actually buttress the functioning of universities everywhere. One characteristic that links universities in mass education countries is enfranchisement of the junior faculty, which is still very limited in Europe. This lack of independence is causing an explosive situation, a major incentive to internal structural reform whose nature is still not adequately recognized in Europe. Universities of all countries have experienced student disturbances, and the net effect of the assault on professorial dominion and of efforts to boost student power is the emergence of young teachers' aspirations.

Failure to consider young academic workers has an ancient tradition. In the administration of the Catholic Church it can be clearly observed in the phenomenon of princely episcopal figures surrounded by faceless but serious young clerks who actually perform the basic chores. Junior university teachers are less visible but no less indispensable. They perform most of the functions of teaching, consulting, and administration, the rewards for which are hopes for eventual professorial preferment and actual day-to-day power over students far out of keeping with their low-level formal status.

Attack on Academic Princes

In an age of democracy, where the battle cry is to share power widely, there is an odd anachronism in the structure of universities, which restrict formal decisions to a veteran gerontocracy while leaving younger staff *de jure*, if not necessarily *de facto*, disenfranchised. This lack of consistency where it exists is the central symbol of internal academic problems. In Europe, and to some extent in Japan and the USSR, the structure of academic governance is out of balance and top-heavy with senior-staff influence over the organizational decision instruments. Hence, many heads are turned toward the USA where a better balance is said to prevail.

American universities are forums of built-in tensions that somehow resolve themselves into cooperation. Senior and junior teachers are relatively united by a common concern about the growing powers of the presidency. Central administration should by definition be weak, since it must preside over employee professors whom it cannot fire. But the coordinating function for which it has been created endows it with a certain resilience. Also, the legal structure favors administration over faculty in several areas of decision-making. In addition, in the United States the diversity of subjects and specialities offered within the walls of the universities is so large and many of the specialities so experimental that great financial superstructures of laboratories, libraries, computers, experimental farms, and sport stadia have built up. To manage such far-flung enterprises, astute administrative and executive talent is required. Presidents of American universities, far from being benign rectors chosen from among equals for short-term representational purposes as in Europe, are forceful figures, skilled (even when selected from among professors) in public relations and fiscal management.

American university presidents are ambivalent about professors. They profess admiration and support for their "colleagues," but secretly they grumble about tenure, faculty absenteeism, and innumerable professorial caprices. Professors are equally ambivalent. On one side they treat their leaders with deference born, no doubt, of a respect for those with political and financial power. On the other, they are forever hostile to administrative presence and jealous about its continued encroachments. The fact that most statutory powers are in the hands of presidents and boards of trustees rather than those of professors does not help matters. The result of all these tensions is relative balance, and though under the impact of student revolts some proposals to weaken the administration by strengthening faculty power have been made and passed, at Columbia University, for instance, these efforts have not been extensive enough to disturb the equilibrium.

In other countries there is no such equilibrium, and in Europe especially current faculty structure with the powers it confers on senior professors has been publicized everywhere as a major abuse. In faculty-type universities all decisions are generated by the chairs. A weak and rotating central administration serves only to rubber stamp them. Yet, the large expansion of mass universities raised new admissions problems and increased the scope of financial operation which professors alone cannot handle. Shared responsibility is demanded by students, by the government, by civic groups, by university administrators and, last but not least, by the totally disenfranchised groups of young teaching staff and research workers. To this pressure the universities have to respond not only in Europe but in Japan and even in the Soviet Union.

So far, response has been expressed in policy statements, planning meetings, and a few experiments. In Europe there have been few actual changes. The possibility of a strong presidency is discussed. A few rectors in Germany now are elected not for one but at least four years, and one or two are permanent, though not yet powerful. The effectiveness of such persons is directly correlated with their academic prestige. The more renowned they are, the more they are listened to, suggesting again the strength of government by senior teachers. In Japan and the USSR, where presidents and rectors are appointed by the government and hold office for indefinite years, great care has been exercised to place these posts in the hands of prominent academics.

In all countries, including the United States, senior men continue to have a lion's share in university government. Those of top rank reign supreme in university affairs if only because in the long run they can be occasionally silenced but never overthrown so long as academic tenure continues to prevail as a system. In spite of constant attacks on tenure on both sides of the Atlantic, it seems to be holding fast. Even in the USSR the quinquennial review is purely formalistic and hardly a major cause of professorial turnover.

Faculty members in all countries have staying power over their temporary rivals. Bodies which attempt to control the universities, whether they be students, alumni, private trustees, municipal agencies, state officials, or religious groups, meet with only partial success. Protected by lifetime positions, by prestige that comes from a high level of specialization, and fundamental devotion to good works, tenured university professors survive the successive flare-ups of criticism, and when the hue and cry dies down, they are still there, the only ones left to carry on.

The sixties witnessed a determined assault on internal university structure. It moved the senior men but little; in fact, it aroused them to join in their own defense. The International Committee on University Emergency (ICUE), formed in New York in 1970, organized professors from fifty-three universities in the USA, Australia, Japan, and several countries of Western Europe to "preserve the autonomy of intellectual and cultural life" and to arrest the process whereby, "increasingly from Berkeley to Berlin, political criteria are being used to evaluate academic performance" (International Committee, 1971, p. 13). As as example of such abuses the Committee pointed out that "in Germany, in some leading faculties, a coalition of students, junior teachers, and nonacademic personnel can out-vote professors on requirements for doctoral examinations." The complaint, one of many, is interesting because it asserts that senior professors are more appropriate persons to decide such requirements. It is hardly likely that such power will be taken away from them on a world scale. But questioning of this and any special authority of chairholders is being heard from many quarters and is at the base of the push for major structural innovations in countries of expanding mass higher education.

Any move toward more balanced administration, especially in Europe, would, in line with American precedents, improve the internal structure. But such reshuffling is merely a symptom of the crisis of confidence that has descended on higher education. Nowhere in the world is there resistance by students to teachers they admire. If the once-inspiring lectures of professors now sound hollow, if assistants and students are not caught up in esprit de corps but feel captives of the system, if dignified subject matter does not uplift but annoys instead, this simply means that professors have lost the erstwhile admiration of their listeners. This phenomenon is worldwide. Murmured criticisms swelling under the lecterns in Moscow are no different from the *hantai* cries in Tokyo. "Treason" is shouted at professors in New York, as it is in Berlin.

A shortcut reason for this reversal of affection is worth stating, though it must be only one of many. In matters of social awareness, which is so well symbolized by the advances of mass higher education, students and junior teaching staff claim jointly that the university has changed too little while society has changed very much. Many historians of universities have written about academic freedom and tenure as devices to protect dissenting professors, suggesting that in the past most professors were dissenting. Actually, most professors have been consenting. A society will tolerate inquiring and even critical professors in the universities, but no sane society would consistently support or tolerate revolutionary teachers. It has never had to, because professors were always an elite, and all elites support systems which support them. By committing themselves to university work professors may be spurning material possessions, but, being sons of the possessing classes themselves, they seldom repudiate the system of which they are beneficiaries.

Thus the charge, particularly fashionable among students in the United States, that professors today have sold out to the system cannot be sustained. In broad generalization professors have always supported the system that is the product of the civilization of which they are guardians. But as societies of men, the universities are not immune from suffering degeneration. Hence, over and over again new forces have to be deployed to bring about their renewal.

A sure index of the decay which brought out the students' revolution is that professors, while supporting the system, do not speak out against its abuses. Too many professors, particularly at senior level, seem to their critics too content to take refuge in narrow research, too willing to train only the very talented, to rationalize away the weaknesses of the system which keeps them at its apex, to acquiesce or abet selfish national policies, and to turn a deaf ear to deprivation and lack of access among the masses. It all began when too many professors kept silent under Nazism and cowed in terror under Stalin's extravagances. Criticism grew into a wholesale outcry when only student violence could compel the academic world to entertain reforms and when war armaments and exploitation at home and the overwhelming needs of the Third World abroad seemed too lightly glossed over by those whose patent duty it is to point out such abuses. Though many pride themselves on having abandoned and a few have actually demolished their ivory-tower attitudes, too many university teachers exhibit lack of concern with contemporary issues and they do so belligerently. This profoundly alienates the junior group.

To attempt a sociological characterization is not to level charges. One ought to think twice before assaulting a learned, persevering, and basically praiseworthy group of professionals such as university professors. Nor can one lightly assume that innovation-mindedness, for lack of which university faculties are now frequently chastized, is really a characteristic they should be expected to exhibit. Universities are as much agents of stability as agents of change, if not more so. A great deal could be said in favor of reluctant reform in an institution expressly created to conserve cherished cultural traditions. And it is no secret that too often young faculty members, having grown older and perhaps sadly mellower, become set in their ways and that, as has been ably put, "those same senior men, the first pioneers, may become as conservative in the preservation of their once new ideas as the old order of professors in the traditional universities" (Perkin, 1969, p. 160). Only from the viewpoint of mass culture is professorial elitism truly saddening because it implies turning people away from fountainheads of knowledge from which no human has the right to bar another fellow human. But even this charge can be somewhat mitigated by remembering that these exclusions are prompted by quite lofty fears that in the hands of the unworthy the treasured field of learning, of which the professor has been appointed guardian, will be in itself debased.

When all is said and done the fact remains that university professors, and European university professors more than those in countries of mass higher education, obstruct rather than facilitate reforms. Nowhere do professors have a good reform record. Preselected from social classes which are of the establishment or drawn into the establishment through their own successes, professors tend to cling to the social as well as the intellectual rewards they enjoy in the universities. Many are willing to experiment and innovate if this will further their fields. Few, unfortunately, recognize that the infusion of raw power from expanded mass admissions will in the long run bring their subjects new vitality. Professors in the USA and Japan are as a group more liberal than members of other professions, while professors in the USSR are politically fairly neutral. In no country are professors enthusiastic about mass explosion. The

groans of anguish emerging from the faculty of the City University
of New York, now committed to open admission and flooded by
students, permit no challenge to this generalization.

Adjusting Teaching and Research

Highly specialized men, who dedicate themselves to an academic life and by implication to a relatively impecunious existence,
understandably prefer to immerse themselves in research and expect
society to protect their study interests. The charge that professors
are cavalier about social issues is powerfully reinforced by the secondary disenchantment with their tendency to value personal study,
reflection, and research more highly than the less exacting business
of mere dissemination.

Contemporary assaults on university teachers often concentrated on their research function. The larger the mass of students,
the greater the pressure for more teaching attention. Hence disputes
about allocation of functions between research and teaching have
a more authentic ring in American universities than in others. In
the USA, as elsewhere, the ideal profile of a university teacher was
and is to research and to teach at the same time. The twentieth
century saw the slow unbalancing but not the breaking up of this
equation until it became the famous "publish or perish" principle.
Only after World War II did the separation between the two functions really come into being and work its way into structure. In
describing the postsecondary panorama available to faculty, an
American report refers to five distinct types of institutions: major
research universities, regional state universities and colleges, private
state universities and colleges, comprehensive state colleges, and
community and private junior colleges (OECD, 1970d, pp. 12–17).
The sequence is in descending order of concentration on research
and in ascending order of concentration on teaching.

Within each American university and college the graduated
sequence of research is again reproduced. From undergraduate college to master's level and doctoral training to postdoctoral work, the
research quotient increases. Research institutes within universities,
although often separate administratively, are part of the system because they are operated by senior professors with a supporting staff

of junior professors, nonteaching research officers, and doctoral students.

The net effect of the explosion of enrollments is to diminish the role of research in the university. The arrival of the mass has made it less and less possible to maintain the ideal of a teacher-researcher. Students of different ability groups crowded into universities are confronted with absentee or busy research professors, with a research orientation which casts umbrage on their practical orientation, and with subject matter conceived in research terms and ill-adapted to their intellectual level and interests. Their demands for more attention to teaching, more relevance, and more flexible appraisals soon begin pushing the university in a more practical direction.

American universities always have had a great deal of flexibility and practical orientation by comparison with their European prototypes. High academic standards have often been threatened by the countless alternatives open to students in an elective system. Now the pressure has become too much, and research has been forced to move away from academic premises. The separate research institutes on campus in which senior staff members isolate themselves still provide some answers, but research is being pursued increasingly in private or governmental agencies off campus, where ex-academics have shelter and opportunity to concentrate on full-time research.

In future the universities of lesser rank and colleges throughout the nation will devote themselves to dissemination, while towering universities of the first rank will tend to specialize in research. Their graduate schools already overshadow their smaller undergraduate colleges, and their senior staff teach very little. Their eyes are on the world at large and on the reputation that the publications of their faculty and their outside services may bring them.

Other mass higher education countries implicate their universities in similar problems but with decreased intensity. Canada has an excellent record of support of university research by the government, especially in sciences and social sciences, but only 20 percent of total research funds is assigned to universities. Soviet and Japanese universities are also somewhat more teaching-oriented than those in the United States. In the Soviet Union publications are a major source of outside income for professors. Since payment is by number of pages printed the incentives for voluminous publications are multiplied. However, many holders of doctoral degrees, which are awarded only for publications, have only one book in print, and much research goes on in the Academy of Sciences, other academies, and various research institutes in which professors hold joint appointments. The separation between teaching and research functions is further accentuated in Japan. Here government- and business-sponsored research accounts for the major part of the national total. In 1964 "of the 381.7 yen billion expended on research that year 243.8 billion yet was spent by private industry, 60.6 billion yen by research institutes, and 77.3 billion yen by universities" (Burn, 1971, p. 238). Within the universities there is an artificial line separating teaching faculties and research institutes and joint appointments to both are less frequent than elsewhere, so that university teachers and university researchers tend to develop separate loyalties.

European professors share with professors of other countries the inclination toward research. Academic standing is everywhere assessed not by successes in teaching but by publications. Since the esteem of their peers is the dearest ambition of professors all over the world, the "care and feeding" of students in all systems tends to have secondary status. But European universities are not pragmatic, not action-oriented organizations constrained by society to serve the acute needs of an expanding student population. Ancient foundations, secure behind corporate walls, endowed or financed on the basis of old tradition, they were preeminently contemplative institutions from which applied research experimentation, like semimanual work, was jealously kept out. Ancient alchemists had to force their entry into higher education via a Royal Society, a Polytechnic, or a Department of Ordonance. Speculative or empirical research, separate from teaching, was always the primary concern of European professors. For instance, the path of promotion for German university teachers, especially the iron-clad requirement for the "second" (docent's habilitation) thesis, meant that all German professors had to prove their worth twice as researchers. Now pure research is being more clearly incorporated in what is taught, and all European universities, new or old, proclaim the need for balance between teaching and research. One of the new German institutions, the University of Konstanz, states proudly that the most striking feature of its research scene is "that the classical place of university research in Germany, the Institute, does not exist" and that this will mean dissemination of the research function to the level of individual professors (Boning and Roeloff, 1970, p. 94).

Research–teaching priorities agitate the universities of all industrial countries. In one accidental sense, Europe and the USA are similar in having dual paths of research and teaching. In the United States, the duality is just emerging as the university road gets widened and traffic on it increases, while in Europe the paths laid out for teaching and research have always tended to be separate and only recently have efforts been made to converge them. Perhaps Europe can skip from a path directly to a superhighway, thus avoiding unnecessary structural complications.

Faculty Recruitment and Rejuvenation

Since the truism that teachers make the schools has never lost its force, efforts to streamline the recruitment, rights and duties, and self-governing powers of faculty are crucial. Restructuring governance by shifting some decision-making power away from senior professors is merely an internal effort at academic smoothness. It does not negate the central proposition that universities can be controlled only by teachers. The real determination of university policies is shaped by ancient traditions of self-government, and though other agencies of society can construct postsecondary schools, without giving them self-government they cannot turn them into universities. The issue, therefore, is not the shape of the structure but the power of different bodies within faculties to govern.

The key to change is the method of recruiting teaching staff. The movement to enfranchise junior sectors of the university community has real potential for eventually altering the structure. The most innovative feature of current university reform is the inclusion of younger constituencies in deciding new professorial appointments. But deliberate efforts to improve selection are seriously influenced by natural preselection. Patterns of achievement vary among different countries, and a somewhat different range of talents is consequently deployed in the universities.

The contrasts between mass education countries and Europe once again suggest themselves. In the United States, where attractions for the talented to enter business and politics are great, this preselection channels nonmanipulative, less outgoing but also more public-minded people into university teaching. Also, the broad-based school system throws up into university teaching a relatively large proportion of the bright sons of the lower middle class. There is, to cite just one example, an uncommonly large proportion of the sons of lower-class immigrant Jewish people among today's American professors. The professorial body thus represents a wide spectrum of social classes. Members of the upper class, who continue to be present, mingle with large numbers of middle-class men and with the unusually able sons of the lower class. The result is an emphasis on performance as the unifying criterion of worth even though the ideal achievement is, by the managerial standards of other organizations, more bookish than administrative.

This broad social preselection is also characteristic, though less so, of other mass higher education countries. In Canada the selection of faculty includes a goodly percentage of US citizens and Englishmen. In the USSR, where half the population was transferred by the revolution from country to town and where sons of the prerevolutionary elite were for a time denied educational opportunity, a large proportion of the sons of the working class now occupies university positions. Furthermore, the preselection process tends to supply nonpolitical, rather conformist and nonpolemical types of people, who can be contrasted not with the business elite as in the USA but with political activists and government bureaucrats. In Japan, until the Second World War, most university positions were held by the sons of the former samurai. It is this class that has inaugurated, under Emperor Meiji, the modernization program. But since the American Occupation there has been an influx of men from the middle class. As the scope of higher education expands, so does the representation of the latter, at least to judge by the complaints about the "lower tone" as well as the left-wing leanings of the professorial body.

Precise empirical data are not available, but a reasonable qualitative impression suggests that European university teachers are socially much more narrowly selected than are those of mass higher education countries. Bright sons of the poor continue to find their way into the universities since teaching, academic and lower, is the most convenient first stepping-stone out of the working classes. But these "Lucky Jims" assimilate assiduously and thus do not change the social context or tone of European faculties, which remain overwhelmingly upper class and hence elitist. Some European sociologists now favor the "social convergence" over the "embourgeoisement" theory of class change. They believe that as modern lower classes push themselves upward the upper classes are simultaneously moving downward toward them. The development of national cultures from regional ones has always been based on convergence rather than on a one-way imposition of the larger unit on the smaller. But if lower- and upper-class cultures now blend as easily as do regional and national cultures, this phenomenon has yet to register itself visibly in the European universities.

Preselection automatically influences selection. The centuries-old guild spirit on which universities were built has been strengthened by principles of academic freedom into an immovable rock, and everywhere university faculties are jealously self-recruiting. Outside Oxford, Cambridge, and a handful of other directly teacher-run universities, all other forms of university government have legally *deprived* professors of this right to self-recruitment, yet de facto selection of new professors remains steadily in the hands of peers.

In the United States state boards of regents and boards of private trustees hold the power of appointment, and life tenure is styled as "appointment during the pleasure of trustees." Yet even university presidents, though increasingly initiators of new appointments, particularly those made on the "reform ticket," are virtually powerless to act against the consensus of the department concerned. In the Soviet Union, with all that has been written about the strength of the Party and the government and its interference in all aspects of life, the centrality of the *Uchonnyi Soviet* (faculty council) as regards new appointments has hardly been touched. In Japan, a veritable war between the Ministry of Education and the University of Tokyo in the early sixties about too unrestricted faculty determination of appointments ended with the university succeeding in retaining its prerogatives. In European countries, in most universities, professors are appointed by the state, yet ministries in

Germany or France and the councils or courts in English universities appoint only candidates proposed by the faculties.

If there is to be a "new wave" of reform-minded professors, it will have to be generated by the faculties themselves. Junior-staff power is clearly the main weapon that can be tried to bring about a more imaginative selection of teachers as an important antidote to the present naturally conservative modes of preselection.

The conversion from the organization of faculties by chairs to an organization by departments is often presented as the heart of this reform by rejuvenation. The former structure concentrates power in the hands of senior tenured staff and consigns overworked, underpaid, and undervalued junior staff to a state of tutelage, who continue to be junior often well into middle age. The contrast with the department structure is vivid. In American universities even instructors—that is, teachers who have yet to earn the doctorate—often participate in the decision-making processes of academic departments. Award of the Ph.D. is usually followed automatically by granting the rank of assistant professor, and such rank, though five to ten years prior to tenure, usually entitles its holder to full participation in departmental affairs.

Although departments can be used to enhance the power of energetic chairmen (Canada, which has partially adopted departmental structure, had to make special provision to increase rotation of administrators)', these difficulties have not prevented the general trend toward departmental organizations. In Japan, faculty structure has been weakened by introduction of general education faculties (offering courses for first- and second-year students)' separate from senior faculties and by conversion to departmental structure in junior colleges. The impact of American practice on universities has been a general weakening of the chairs. In the USSR the *Kafedra* (chair) continues to be the basis of organization, but chairs and faculties exist side by side with departments, depending on specialty and university. Because of the extensive regulation of budgets, curricula, and appointments by the Ministry of Higher Education relatively few powers are left in the hands of chairholders.

In Europe, too, conversion to department structure is a clear trend. In France, in Germany, and in Denmark, to mention only a few measures have been taken at several universities to effect such a change. However, in many cases the new organization did not imply a real innovation. The University of Bochum in Germany, for instance, was organized expressly to be a trailblazer in fostering department structure, yet only a few years after its founding Boning and Roeloff (1970, p. 75) characterized the reform as follows:

The main novelty in the internal structure of Bochum is the division into 18 departments instead of the traditional larger faculties. For the administrative organisation and the structure of academic self-government, however, it has had surprisingly little consequences. In fact, the structure plan points out very clearly that the purpose of the new departments is indeed to reestablish the original function of the faculties under modern conditions with regard to the organisation of science and research; it states with equal clarity that the 18 departments as units for university policy and administration are to function as 18 faculties again. Following strict logic the professors of one department are again called "Fakultät." . . . The heads of the 18 departments are constitutionally exactly like the "Dekane" of the classical faculties except they are more numerous.

The difficulty of achieving true reform through structural change is also exemplified in another observation by these authors (pp. 82–83):

It may almost seem surprising that Konstanz, definitely the most innovative German university at present, should have maintained the traditional and much criticized sub-division of the university into faculties. One of the reasons was the fear that division of the larger faculties into departments of the Bochum type might result in the creation of more smaller "faculties," thus multiplying the obstacles to reform, cooperation and integration. Thus founders preferred to retain the traditional pattern, but to change its internal structure and re-arrange the weight of the various units in the different spheres according to modern needs.

Instead of departments Konstanz resorted to formation of subject groups within the faculties. The superiority of curricular over administrative innovations seems reflected in the fact that although such subject groups were created in the interest of academic work, accidentally these new groupings have "drained the traditional faculties of a good deal of their traditional power" (p. 83).

The attempt to create departments is not the only means whereby senior-faculty power is being restricted. One method, already mentioned, is to strengthen presidential administration. Two other devices to expand the number of participants in policy-making are being experimented with in Europe and Canada: one is to change the composition of the all-powerful university senates, the official forum and repository of professorial government; another is to create supplementary bodies to split the monopoly held by the senates.

The assault on the composition of the university senates has been intensified in all countries where students have staged revolutions. But even before this, tensions against oligarchic senates were steadily accumulating. In England, there was "tension within the academic staff, between the professors, who had shrunk from a majority to a tiny minority of the faculty, but retained all academic power in senate, and the now large majority of non-professors, who did most of the teaching and research but had, under charters and statutes which scarcely recognized their existence, hardly any rights or powers at all" (Perkin, 1969, p. 140). As a result of such tensions most senates have been democratized.

The issue of strong senior faculty versus other constituent parts of the university was also faced on the level of diversification of organization. The older universities were organized in a strictly *linear* fashion. The flow of authority was based on vertical dependence of the levels of governance on each other. The rector and the senate, the dean of faculty and faculty council, the chair and the chairholder's "own chaps" (as junior staff are euphemistically called in England) could be pictured on a chart as a series of neatly superimposed cubes. To break this linear dependence, parallel organs of governance have been introduced. In some German universities, for instance, the senate has become a two-part unit, the little senate serving as an executive committee of the big senate. An increased role has also been given to the general student committee. The chancery (office of a *Kanzler*) and the kuratorium (office of *Kurator*) within new German universities have been given new prominence in administrative affairs, either under the rector or parallel to the rector.

Thus, we may say that while the details of reforms are genuinely intimate to each situation and while many reforms have yet to be tested by time, the university system based on faculties rather than departments is slowly losing its hold. Insofar as this will mean decentralization of responsibility, all systems of the world are moving in the American direction. Conversion to departments in Europe and admission of students to decision-making bodies in Canada have just begun, and the future will decide their momentum. But it is interesting to note that while Europe is deliberating, in the United States the department structure is being accused of the same rigidity as that charged against European faculties.

From Students to Academic Apprentices

The essence of the new politics concerning teachers is weakening senior professors and strengthening students, thus converging power toward the center where junior professors hold court. While young faculty attempt to "defrock" the chairholders, their allies, the students, are being rewarded for their support by political and intellectual elevation. The university is too stubborn an organization to yield directly to student demands, but it is forced to blunt the impact of their demands by granting enfranchisement to junior teachers to win all young people over to its side. In their bid for power the students will be able to move only half way. The net effect will be that they will be treated with circumspection, not as pupils but as academic apprentices. Thus while outside their walls the universities face the rise of nonuniversity institutions, inside the walls they must now accommodate student aspirations. While junior faculty power is the first, student power is the second wave of university rejuvenation.

Student discontent with the university status quo is an ancient phenomenon that dates to the *gaudeamus igitur* revelries in countless beer cellars. Student revolts in the sixties became front-page news largely because of their particular intensity and the world scale on which they occurred. Several other characteristics distinguish these eruptions from their predecessors. For the first time, the edge of discontent was turned inward, not only against misgovernment of societies but against mismanagement of universities. Anglo-Saxon students who never rioted before came out in demonstrations to bely their long quiescence and lack of interest in university governance. Students in communist countries took part in national revolutions in Poland, Hungary, and Czechoslavakia. In the USSR, from which it is difficult to obtain data, their restlessness manifested itself in rebellious poetry, in questioning government restriction of freedom in fine art, in resenting victimization of unorthodox writers. In Japan and the United States, where the hand of the government rests much more lightly on the universities, the entire society was deeply shaken by occupation of university buildings, boycott of classes, large-scale street demonstrations, and even deaths, providing the student movement with its tragic martyrs. The disturbances in these two countries were probably not unrelated, and the American and Japanese eruptions—and even more the influence of American writers such as Marcuse—had something to do with fomenting European ferment. From Berlin to Paris, from Coimbra to Athens the chain reaction was spontaneous. European disturbances cannot be contrasted with those in mass higher education countries. Everywhere the latent forces were the same, in spite of the variety of manifest causes. Everywhere university students expressed their rebellion against their political elders and made a bid for a share of the internal governance of the academy.

Student demands have a great impact on the public mind but much less "real" effect. In actual fact responses to their demands can be classed as tokenism: instead of full representation they get partial representation, instead of reorganization of courses of study, apparent reorganization. In the end student revolts can act only as reform boosters. Students can start a revolution, but they graduate too fast to be able to preside over its execution.

Reforms brought about by student power can be divided into major groups. First, patterns of student participation in administrative decision-making are being altered, and they do have an impact on changes in the university structure itself. Second, student power has affected their academic as distinct from their political position with favorable redefinitions of student discipline and of study streams geared more to student needs than to maintaining high standards of academic subjects.

Historically, participation of students in university government has depended on the way the universities were formed. In universities following the Bologna pattern—the students federated and hired the masters to further their education—they had a measure of self-government. Latin American universities provide the most complete models of such tradition. But the one-third vote enjoyed there by students at all levels is somewhat neutralized by the fact that the second third belongs to alumni. These usually support the professors, giving the adults a permanent majority. All over Europe, however, it was the Paris pattern of federation of masters who admitted students, rather than students who hired masters, that prevailed. With the exception of Scotland, where students still have the right to elect rectors in an open meeting, very few governing rights were accorded them. Student organizations have been politically strong in Germany and Scandinavia but they had at best only an informal influence within the universities. Internal powers and reach of European student self-government even in the outstanding case of the *Burschenschaften* (German student fraternities) have never been, one suspects, as extensive as those of Student bodies in the USA and are far less influential than the extensive presence of the government-sponsored *Komsomol* in the life of Soviet or the *Zenga-kuren,* the turbulent student union in the life of Japanese universities.

The revolutions of the sixties began a corrective movement. As a result many higher education systems in Europe and a few outside Europe have made or are making provision to include students in the machinery of university government. In Germany "most universities are working out plans to meet the demand [for a greater share of self-government], though none is willing to do so completely (Boning and Roeloff, 1970, pp. 140–141). So far, two student representatives in the senate and in faculty assemblies is a commonly preferred solution. In the United Kingdom, no universities of the 1960s made "specific provision in the Charters or Statutes for student representation on Court, Council or Senate (or their equivalent) although in revised Charters and Statutes currently being negotiated for some older universities, such as Manchester, such provision was being made in the case of Court" (Perkin, 1969, p. 199)'. The new universities Keele and Stirling have made such provision, and elsewhere an increased informal consultation between administration and students prevails. Yugoslavia has had a more regularized system of representation of students in councils of all levels. They have full voting rights in financial decisions "though not those regarding the salaries of the teaching staff" (Institute for Social Research, 1970, p. 127).

There are strong indications for the seventies that negotiations for one-half parity, as in Denmark, or one-third parity, as in Germany, will fail and that even token participation of students in the main decision-making bodies as in Canada will not spread to all countries and all universities. Most proposals for reorganizing universities mention student participation, but one has a feeling that enthusiasm for the implementation of such policies is lacking. In Japan this sentiment has recently been expressed in an official document: "When well qualified student representatives are elected by a free and fair majority vote of students in each election unit, they can participate as formal members of advisory organs of decision making bodies, or of organs taking part in decision making through preliminary discussions. However, students are not sufficiently competent to participate in final decision making bodies or to reject the decisions by such bodies" (OECD, 1970e, p. 7).

In other countries feelings of reluctance and even veiled hostility toward student aspirations, though less openly expressed, are nonetheless also present. Thus, in England, the faculty is declared the "only guardians of the rights of students yet unadmitted," and a plea for limited cogovernment has been expressed in terms of the inappropriateness of the more temporary members, the students (three or four years), having power to legislate matters of vital interest to the less temporary members, the faculty (thirty or forty-five years). "If changes are to be made which may affect the physical layout of the institution and the material comfort of the inhabitants for many years to come, the permanent members have a right to insist that they should not be undertaken lightly, or at the whim of some small and irresponsible group who will not have to suffer the consequences" (Perkin, 1969, p. 198).

However, a real change has occurred at the level of informal consultation, partly out of fear of further revolts and partly out of the genuine desire of teachers to meet the young half way. Teachers are often truly fond of teaching and possess broader sympathies and understanding for the students than do other adults, and perhaps the balance of feeling has in recent years swung in favor of the young. Militant groups of student activists are few in number and transitory, but they impress themselves powerfully on policy-makers through an implied threat of violent disagreement. The rank and file of students sensitized by these activities to political issues tend to be less absorbed than they used to be in studies and job preparation, less willing to accept unquestioningly courses of study presented to them, and more likely to seek confrontation on controversial issues.

The result is a growing system of consultation. Students now govern their student unions and refectories, participate in designing curriculum, and are responsible for student discipline. In the United States student opinions are sought on financing, on programs, and most significantly on election and promotion of teaching staff. This consultation may be expected to increase not only because students may demand it but because students can be valuable allies of the faculty in their struggles with trustees and presidents.

In Europe student participation is spreading southward from Scandinavia, where even in administrative decision-making it is very extensive. In Yugoslavia there are now informal student-teacher committees in which the two parties coordinate common policy. In Germany, as exemplified by Bochum, the student welfare bureau (*Studentenwerke*) disburses national funds for stipends, health cures, and meal tickets. In England most student bodies meet on a regular basis with university administration, and at several places, notably the new universities, students are in charge of internal discipline. In France, student participation is an essential part of the Orientation Law of 1968. The effects of the sixties are least evident in the USSR and Japan, in the former because there were no student disturbances to speak of, in the latter, oddly enough, because there were too many disturbances. These caused the alignment of the public with the authorities against the students.

Quite a significant change in faculty-student relations lies not in the area of power but in the area of status. There is an almost universal tendency to abandon the in loco parentis doctrine. This problem varies, of course, with the locale of the university. Residential schools, schools for girls, or schools for younger undergraduates always adopted a stricter attitude toward student behavior than have metropolitan, coeducational, or graduate institutions. In the United States, in the celebrated Barnard College case in 1965, a girl student who was "living in sin" with her boyfriend received the mild punishment of a three-week suspension of cafeteria privileges, handed down by a faculty-student board. Across the country the parietal rules restricting mutual visits to dormitories have completely disappeared. In England the Committee on the Age of Majority commented: "There will no longer be a vague conviction that a college should look after a student in every personal way, no longer a misty territory where it is clear that the Dean does not make a man cut his toenails and does make him sit his exams, but most things in between are a matter of dispute" (Report, 1967, p. 403). It can be predicted that restrictions such as overnight passes, curfews, regulations as to specific dress, and even compulsory attendance at lectures will in time disappear. Disciplinary measures will require "due process." The status of students as independent young adults will replace the *in statu pupillari* situation. The treatment of students as if they were school infants is a vital contributory cause of the present wave of indignation.

Efforts are also being made to clarify students' intellectual status. This change means a conversion from regarding students as pupils in an academic as well as in a disciplinary sense to admitting them to the rights of junior academic colleagues. In line with these innovations are efforts to improve access of students to teachers, including the maintenance of a small ratio of students per professor and attacks on absenteeism and aloofness of professors. The larger the university system the more insistent the demand that professors act as teachers. Thus in Germany expansion of staff, especially at the junior level, is followed by "organization of introductory courses, guidance and tutoring groups; the coordination of lecture courses with discussion groups for preparation and evaluation; the setting up of detailed study programmes and examination requirements for interim and final examinations, and improvement of the mechanism to assure a corresponding organization of courses; the introduction of team teaching; the improvements in the library system" (Boning and Roeloff, 1970, p. 115).

Attempts are also being made to convert lectures to seminars at all new English, French, and German universities. However, some reports from Germany indicate that students tend to cling to the lecture system and from England that, even in the new universities, a vast majority of students tend to favor it. Similarly, talk-and-chalk lectures persist even in the United States, though that country has long insisted on active student discussion and instruction in small groups and seminars.

The small tutorial and guidance system is a further extension of the trend toward individualization. In the United States the guidance system of secondary schools is extended via tutors and section men into college and via the faculty adviser into graduate schools. Apart from the tutorial system at Oxford and Cambridge, this type of close attention to students has not been widespread in European or Soviet and Japanese universities. Recently "moral tutors" have appeared at the new English universities, and in Germany "guidance and counselling are intensified and institutionalized" (Boning and Roeloff, 1970, p. 115). Though this "tailor-made" treatment of students is still not common, and it will be some time before it is universal, at least efforts are being made to do away with "the misunderstandings which separated teachers from students, the impossibility of establishing a real 'dialogue' and the absence of 'exchanges'—in short, the mutual incomprehension of pedagogical partners" (Grignon and Passeron, 1970, p. 10).

UNYIELDING UNIVERSITY CURRICULUM

6

While numbers in mass higher education are exploding and junior teachers are rising, the social composition of the student body is standing fairly still. The curriculum shares a similar fate. Most innovations outside the USA, especially in European universities, are structural, hard reforms. The pressure of numbers has not reached the curricular, soft reforms. The weight of the past is so great that few think of meeting or anticipating emergencies by modernizing the subjects offered. Raised in centralized traditions and habituated to bureaucratic regulation of abuses, the Soviets and Japanese join with Europeans in believing that content is determined by structure. They do not share the easygoing North American optimism that content will generate organization and that the less regularized the structure the less oppressed and obstructed the spontaneously emerging contents. Even if they wanted to reform, until they strike down the formal edifice they cannot liberalize content. They are forced, therefore, to fumble with the structure first, in order perhaps later to gain freedom to enjoy American flexibilities.

In the old universities of Europe, subject matter had little direct relation to structure. In each university, faculties as theoretical as philosophy were established side by side with faculties as specific as medicine; in spite of different purposes their faculty organizations were identical. In lower levels of education, in the guilds, too, glovers had not much to do with apothecaries, but the structures of their respective professional systems remained essentially the same.

The proliferation of specialities made close relation between content and structure more likely. The particular needs of each field demanded administration suited to its purpose. The gap between apprenticeship and formal schooling began to be filled from both sides. At the lower level, different specialities acquired formal courses of study and grew into full-scale institutions, such as technical universities or institutes of fine arts. At the higher level, new specialities kept being added to the old academic faculties until the university became a veritable conglomerate uneasily held together by a federal overstructure. "University," an American university president once quipped, "is a series of independent departments loosely united by plumbing."

Curricular innovations have as their theme the conversion of professors' loyalty to their own subjects into broad participation in planning for the university as a whole. This change is never easy and it is hardest within firmly entrenched traditional university structures. Curricular victories of the past have, in Europe, been so institutionalized that no further innovations can be contemplated without first attacking the structure. Thus, outside the USA university reformers content themselves with a few attempts to sneak in new approaches to subject matter via structural means, through the back door, as it were. Though content revision is vital to accommodate properly the variety of talents that are appearing in mass universities, such measures are simply postponed or at least kept in low key until the forbidding academic redoubts have been appropriately dismantled.

Resistance to Reform

Postsecondary levels of European-type university education are dominated by hallowed traditions. The earliest establishments

of the *studium generale* were frankly contemplative or narrowly professional. They contained and still retain groups of people whose
purpose in life was sheer reflection, as evidenced by the overwhelming number of clerics. When religion became laicized and scholastic
disputes not only acquired theological meaning but became tools
to teach "white-collar workers," the university became a forum for
training in argument. This purpose suited lawyers, administrators,
a few other professionals, and no more. Outside these narrow con-
fines of medieval professionalism there were only medicine and perhaps astronomy, but even in these infant sciences, learning scholastic argument held sway over laboratory experience. Until the
eighteenth century, the field of higher education held nothing else.

These ancient facts remind the reader that university traditions are based on a humanistic, verbal, and narrowly professional
orientation and that the age of science, which hit the world of
higher education in the eighteenth and nineteenth centuries, has
even now not totally come into its own. Although more than 80
percent of students at Moscow University are enrolled in the sciences, more than three-quarters of Oxford students are in the humanities. Even within these concentrations the choices are narrow.
As an English authority put it in personal correspondence: "It has
always seemed to me quite extraordinary that we in this country
should be doubling and redoubling our University population and
still be reluctant to accept courses which fall short of an early
twentieth century concept of academic scholarship. There is, I believe, only one university course in English and Drama in Britain
and this has 50 applicants for every place. Meanwhile, courses in
English which are essentially courses in literary criticism proliferate.
Far from providing higher education associated with plumbing or
butchery we do not even have courses in journalism or accoun-
tancy."

The curriculum in all countries of mass higher education,
even in the USA, is changing very slowly, and in Europe it has
scarcely budged, even in the most innovative countries such as England or Sweden. There is very little doubt that it is the universities
which resist the change. All around the universities training facilities for all sorts of callings are being provided, as they always have
been, by on-the-job training, by apprenticeship, by short training

courses, and by longer, more formalized courses and institutions. But the attitude of the universities is crucial to curricular innovations, for what happens outside the universities acquires permanent standing only when it is recognized as worth including or equal in depth to university training. The growing number and sophistication of studies outside the universities are not matched by recognition of these changes inside.

The United States is readiest with such recognition, as witness the speedy recent inclusion of African studies in the curriculum. In the Soviet Union the institutes and technicums provide a channel for institutionalizing curricular changes. Japan and Europe are most reluctant to innovate. The French have formulated this resistance in a manner applicable to all universities: "Insofar as the university has a function of cultural conservation and consecration, 'canonization proceedings' take some time, varying in duration according to the discipline. The period that elapses before an educational innovation wins general academic acceptance may, incidentally, be an effective indicator of the degree of *university inertia* in the various disciplines. While this timelag is tending to disappear in mathematics and physics, it is more noticeable in biology and medicine; but it is longer in law and longest still in the arts or philosophy disciplines" (Grignon and Passeron, 1970, p. 96).

Several symptoms of curricular inflexibility can be identified. First, we may refer to the so-called map of learning, which reveals in countries outside the USA a rigid hierarchy composed of four broad categories: the traditional subjects (philosophy, Greek, Latin, medieval linguistics, law), the modern subjects, sciences, and finally other subjects. This classification is not only according to type but according to scale of prestige, a relief of the terrain as it were, hence the reference to the map. European sources, especially, are full of evidence of the ways "nobler" subject dominate and limit the freedom of others.

The traditional subjects, rooted in the dignified Greco-Roman heritage from which the universities sprang, rule almost unchallenged today, as they have for centuries. This "gerontocracy of disciplines" permits the philosophers to prevail in most academic decisions. In France "the relations between such disciplines as psychology or sociology and philosophy are still influenced, even in the manner of teaching these two sciences, by the traditional hierarchy which tends to bring the latest offspring of anthropological research before the patriarchal tribunal of philosophy" (Grignon and Passeron, 1970, p. 97). In Germany, even at Aachen, which is one of the more forward-looking universities, the test of success in fostering innovations is that "the common sense of the technologist is catching even for the philosophy people" (Boning and Roeloff, 1970, p. 67). The predominance of older subjects, a logical outcome of cherished traditions, has lent much dignity to the universities, but it has made the academy supremely unsuited to foster deliberate curricular modernization.

A prime example of the effect of this inflexible hierarchy is the fate of educational studies in Europe, where in most countries the chair of pedagogy continues to be placed directly within the faculty of philosophy. As a result, compared to the veritable torrent pouring out of the USA, Canada, Japan, and the USSR, studies of educational science in European universities are few. It is startling that professional study of the subject which is most strongly affected by recent turbulence should be in the countries of Rousseau, Pestalozzi, and Piaget restricted so severely by control of the most conservative faculties. In mass education countries, with the USSR as a hybrid case, faculties of education have long been independent. Either as graduate schools within the universities or as independent institutes of education of university rank, these faculties have taken hold of the teaching profession and wield formidable power unparalled by any comparable influence in Europe.

Modern subjects—history, living foreign languages, and all other subjects that have worked their way into the universities in the nineteenth century following the *Realschule* movement—also maintain in Europe a conservative rather than a liberal stance. Although some creative writing in history has been characterized by the social consciousness that originated in the age of Elia Halevy in France and R. H. Tawney in England, European historians have so far employed little sociological analysis, unlike their American colleagues. Audio-visual methods pioneered in the USA by foreign-language specialists are also not widespread. In Europe modern subjects do not include behavioral sciences and act as allies of the older disciplines in maintaining their sacred supremacy.

In the sciences "crossing the Snow line,"—that is, bridging the celebrated gap between the two cultures of the arts and the sciences dramatized by Lord Snow—has become fashionable in the new universities of England and Germany. But the arduous battle for admission the sciences fought is still not over. The sciences tower in Soviet universities and they are growing strong in the USA and Canada but not in Japanese universities. In European universities they were historically relegated to a lesser place, partly, no doubt, because of the existence of first-rate and high-ranking separate technical establishments.

Many other subjects are either denied entrance or have to fight for acceptance. Anthropology and other behavioral sciences have to "plead their cause and prove their worth before a 'family council,' " and they tend to concentrate on "the study of precursors or classical 'founding fathers' whose authority is recognized by the traditional disciplines: this is a characteristic attitude of a disputed discipline which is unsure of its intellectual legitimacy" (Grignon and Passeron, 1970, p. 97). The less historical the specialization the more strongly applied are the rules of exclusion and legitimization. The wholescale turmoil induced in European universities by student revolts remarkably has not resulted in any major changes in the traditional subject hierarchy. Precedence of older subjects and the need to legitimize the new also haunt the mass higher education universities, but their traditional curricular positions have been seriously undermined and the stage is set for further democratization.

A second symptom of curricular inflexibility is the gap between the mental and manual pursuits of man, which has not been reduced by traditional universities at all. Even "ornamental" subjects such as fine arts, music, and sports, which flourish in and out of American universities and which have made heavy inroads into patterns of higher education in the USSR and to some extent in Japan, have not found their way into European university thinking, even in a tentative fashion. Subjects such as architecture, engineering, and business appear in mass higher education countries within university walls as a consequence of diversification forced by mass age. Yet they have made little impact on most European universities, and even less can one expect the appearance, some might say mercifully, of courses in animal husbandry or home economics. These subjects, like any other intellectually honest form of human activity, to paraphrase Jerome Bruner, could be bases for higher levels of intellectual endeavor. Driver education courses can be used as openers for the sociology of urban traffic or the study of combustion engines. Animal husbandry can lead to chemistry and genetics. What mass education countries offer as a lesson to their traditional partners is the infinite value of capitalizing or all facets of human ingenuity.

Another element in the unwieldiness of traditional curricula is the long duration of university studies. In mass education countries the trend is to shorten the length of study. In Western Europe, although the need to curtail duration is now recognized, the tendency in practice has been to lengthen it. Conscious attempts in Europe to shorten study time have not been very successful and the disparity between theoretical and real duration of studies is increasing. As the university fills with students who are not sufficiently prepared to tackle it, their only remedy is to stay in school longer and to work harder. University professors are unwilling to cut out old knowledge. As new knowledge appears it must simply be added, and this demand to digest ever more material, combined with the requirement of high standards and the encyclopaedic approach, also tends to lengthen the years spent in the universities.

"Between 1960 and 1965 in Germany, Denmark and the Netherlands only about 30 percent of graduates succeeded in acquiring their diplomas in the prescribed time." And in Yugoslavia and France only 15 percent of graduates accomplished this goal. "There exists in all institutions a marked disparity between the theoretical course of studies which has been fixed by the legislator and the real course which requires a much longer time to complete" (OECD, 1971a). It is not clear whether this disparity is due primarily to top-heavy academic curriculum or to economic stress which may drive students to interrupt their studies. Research in a few universities in countries such as the Netherlands or Belgium suggests that undue prolongation of studies results in a greatly lowered success rate.

In mass education countries technology and new insights into learning processes prompt the constant repackaging of learning materials. Increased efficiency makes it possible to offer the same bulk in shorter periods of study. Some of the bulk, too, is jettisoned as useless or not relevant. The result is a tendency to reorganize frequently and to lower the age at which subjects are learned. The Ford Foundation–sponsored Advanced Placement Program in college and similar programs elsewhere have established a precedent for a lowered college entrance age. At the Ph.D. level, reports such as the Elder Report at Harvard and the Barzun Report at Columbia call for shortening the permitted length of study so as to eliminate the eternal student and increase the output of Ph.D.s. Most recently "Less Time, More Options" was adopted as a motto by the Carnegie Commission on Higher Education (1971).

The trend toward reorganization and shortening is manifest also in the USSR and Japan. In the former, length of secondary schooling was recently reduced from eleven to ten years. A dramatic shift of the entire syllabus has made first-graders study second-grade materials and so on up. The university course, like that in Europe, has held fast to five years, but in its more flexible offshoots, such as educational studies, many five-year courses have been revised to fit in four years. The study programs of the technicums also remain flexible, from one and a half to three and a half years. In Japan the conversion of higher education from the European to the American pattern after World War II has shortened the longer educational courses to four years. The junior colleges, inaugurated soon after, introduced alternatives of two- or three-year programs. In 1969 the Central Education Council, through its Twenty-Sixth Committee dealing with reforms of higher education, recommended that the length of study be flexible rather than uniformly four years. Though the result of this innovation cannot be predicted with certainty, shorter study courses will undoubtedly develop in at least some specialities. "The general acceptance of the need in Japan to restructure the university system is based on the general awareness of the need for a new flexibility" (OECD, 1970g, p. 39).

Although some European universities have been forced to hold constant or even to expand the length of studies, as we have mentioned, attempts to move in the opposite direction also are being made. In Holland, for example, the Posthumus Report of 1969 recommended shortening all university courses, now variously between four and a half years and seven years, to four years (Snyders,

1970, p. 9)'. Similar recommendations were made in Germany, but as in Holland they have so far had little effect. In Yugoslavia enactment of the university reforms of 1958 to 1962 resulted in slight reduction of periods of studies in various institutions (OECD, 1971a)'. Only the British university undergraduate course, as well as most nonuniversity courses, remained both in theory and in practice short, that is, three years. This British pattern has not been due to the impact of mass higher education, but its results certainly argue for reduced university courses in general: although British students obtain their first degree after a period of study which is much shorter, often by one-half, than that of students elsewhere in Europe, "the level atttained (in Britain) is nevertheless very comparable" (OECD, 1971a).

These indicators—the resistance to change of the old inegalitarian hierarchy of subjects, persisting prestige differences between mental and manual talent, and the tendency unofficially to lengthen the time of study—are among several factors validating the judgment that curriculum reforms in European higher education have in most cases not yet, under the impact of numbers, reached the take-off point long passed by the United States and now being reached by Canada, Japan, and the Soviet Union.

Interdisciplinary Efforts

Despite indications of procrastination, one must guard against overdrawing the picture of inactivity in European university curriculum development. Although they have been kept out of the university, a number of specializations are flourishing and are expanding as creatively in Europe as in mass countries.

The most vividly positive curricular activity which Europe shares with the other countries is the creation of interdisciplinary generalized courses. This innovation is the easiest to put across because it is in reality a structural as well as a curricular reform, and European universities are on the verge of substantial structural reorganization. The prevailing faculty system, which favors immediate professional specialization, is based on a strong, general secondary school. Even the more specialized British sixth form, because of its historically elitist character, is able to furnish university candidates with strong general backgrounds who are capable of immediate specialization. But the expanded numbers in the secondary systems have had the usual short-range effect of weakening, at least in terms of traditional university requirements, the standard general preparation expected.

Thus, the universities of Europe are faced with what American and Japanese universities have faced when hit by expansion of numbers—the need for a remedial general education year prior to specialized university study. The Harvard Report on General Education in a Free Society inaugurated two-year general education courses in many American universities and influenced their partial introduction in others. Expansion of numbers by itself would tend to drive European universities in this direction. But in addition, innovations aimed at interdisciplinary organization of studies are helpful in assaulting the conservative chair system; they are devices to get at the structure via the curriculum.

Interdisciplinary efforts are being made in several countries, both at the all-university level and at the faculty level, and many students demanded more of them in recent demonstrations. But on the whole, these attempts have been tentative and it is by no means clear whether they will succeed in breaking down the dividing lines between faculty subject interests. "The most striking feature of new institutions of higher learning," reports an OECD document (1967a, p. 9), "and the most apparent deviations from the traditional pattern lie in this field: creation of interdisciplinary programs, combined degrees; obligation or possibility for students to take courses belonging to different disciplines (major, minor supporting subjects); obligation or possibility for teachers to belong to two, or more constituent units of the University."

Joseph Ben-David (n.d., p. 64), in another searching OECD report, comments on "interdisciplinary research units with training functions at a number of British, French and German universities." But he cautions that the prevailing satisfaction of the universities with the status quo is unlikely "to institute basic changes." "The universities are rigid organizations, unhospitable to fields where there are no venerable systems and texts." Grignon and Passeron also complain that "interdisciplinary studies have so far led to eclectic patchwork and not to the full and entire recognition of really new intermediate disciplines." The examples they cite tell their own story:

> *Educational organization juxtaposes modern linguistics and the classical type of philosophy without permitting the latter to unify a varied field which, as far as the student is concerned, remains the private tilting-ground of teachers. Similarly, comparative literature has indeed been introduced into the Faculties, but its synthesizing purpose has somehow become "encysted" and thereby denied, insofar as the traditional language and literature courses between which it might have woven new links have succeeded in isolating it in its role of additional special subject thus destined to be rapidly absorbed into the routine [1970, p. 97].*

More enthusiastic reports on the successes of interdisciplinary studies come from the new universities in Britain, deliberately set for innovations and supported by the British experimental tradition. The Foundation Year at Keele in which students prepare for specialized training by studying topics crosscutting humanities, social sciences, and natural sciences has been judged, in spite of complaints about some of its features, very successful in developing student confidence in handling intellectual subjects (Perkin, 1969, p. 118). The Keele innovation strongly influenced other new universities. Some version of "open courses," an "arts-science scheme," or a "school of studies" appears in all new British universities except Stirling. But even English enthusiasts have reservations about extending the interdisciplinary principle to the universities at large.

> *As a solution for the range of problems presented by too early and too narrow specialization, broader curricula and interdisciplinary studies are not necessarily adequate in themselves. The traditional general arts or general science degree at pass level, until recent years the commonest degree in many civic universities, is now generally admitted to have been useless for this purpose. It offered the student the worst of both worlds: a collection of diluted honors courses taught in watertight compartments, individually inadequate to make him a stimulating and synthesizing generalist. The old general pass degree was held to be inferior to the specialized honors*

degree because it was inferior in practice. In recent years, beginning with the general honors degree in arts at Birmingham University in 1947 and continuing with the "science greats" course at Manchester, there has been some attempt to integrate and to give meaning and purpose to the general degree at many of the civic universities, and to raise the standard to honors level. Yet the problem remains in all departmental universities that the departments will be tempted to devote most of their time and attention to "their own" students on the single-subject (or, at best, dual-subject) honors courses, while it remains no one's responsibility (save that of an overworked tutor to general degree students, perhaps) to see that the various combinations of general degree courses add up to an integrated, meaningful education with a clear-sighted aim and purpose.

And as long as general degree students are taught, as they still commonly are, in separate classes, often by separate staff, they will be regarded, like the lower streams of streamed secondary schools, as second-class citizens [Perkin, 1969, p. 116].

These interdisciplinary difficulties are a worldwide phenomenon. In Soviet universities curricula are strictly organized by subjects and specializations. Recent reductions in the number of specializations from over two hundred to ninety has forced some consolidation of subject matter. Compulsory lectures in Marxism-Leninism provide a sociopolitical integrative vehicle for all students. But beyond this, study courses are strictly single-subject. In Japan general studies for the first two years of college have not had a smooth history. Like the social studies which replaced the now-restored course in morals in lower schools, these subjects were never fully understood by Japanese teachers and never acquired the depth and precision that would eventually bring them prestige equal to that of specialized studies. The principle of general education is less in trouble in the United States. Being an innovation proposed by Americans, it "took" there, even though as *studium generale* it has an ancient European tradition. Interdisciplinary arrangements of all sorts in any case predate general education and thrive in several forms: elective curriculum for all students; joint professorial appointments—interfaculty and increasingly interuniversity; closely meshed joint study programs; and interdisciplinary seminars and

research teams. The prevalence of these arrangements makes it difficult to define the source of knowledge acquired and may lower standards of specialization, but the system has buoyancy and enables
constantly changing but exciting combinations of competence to be
brought to bear on common subjects of interest.

Unrealized Potential

A final glance at the comparative curriculum picture in
Western Europe reveals the absence of several types of curricular
innovations that occupy an important place in North American universities and to a lesser degree also in the USSR and Japan. The
following examples, culled from the recent reform experience of
mass education countries, describe reforms which have not been
central to the world of European higher education.

Work-Study Schemes. The notion that theoretical studies
should be accompanied by practice is as old as the sciences or the
apprenticeship system. In modern school theory it stems from Europe, where George Kerschensteiner originated the *Arbeitschule* at
lower school levels. At the university level in Europe this tradition
is rare, except in Britain where sandwich courses and part-time
study have been common in postsecondary education for a long
time. But vast implementation of this concept exists in mass education countries. In the United States the tradition embodied by Anti-
och College is a century old, yet formally, only a few universities,
such as Northeastern in Boston, have officially implemented this tradition in curriculum. It is most widespread in such special fields as
practice-teaching or training of nurses or agriculture. It is almost
universal in the informal custom which permits students to take
jobs—even children of the rich make it a point of honor to "put
themselves through school" by waiting on tables, working summers,
or pumping gas. In Canada 30 percent of all student income comes
from earnings (Burn, 1971, p. 110). In Japan students similarly
devote a portion of time to *Arbeit,* or work to gain economic support.

But the major model of work-study schemes in the universities is found in the Soviet Union, where the 1958 reform attempted
with partial success to shift school and university programs radically
into the field of application. All university courses were ordered to

provide "practical activities" if they already did not have them. Summer work, such as agricultural colonization of Kazakhstan, was officially organized and encouraged. Not all the reforms introduced proved lasting, but half of all students take correspondence courses and more attend evening university courses, thus combining work and study. Although the Soviet correspondence courses seem recently to have gone into decline, there are still few systems which approach Soviet work-study programs. Most recently China has distinguished itself by setting up schemes whereby adult intellectuals as well as students do manual work by rotation.

In most countries deliberate work-study schemes are provided in teacher-training, in archeology, and in other specialties in which laboratory or field work is required. But university degree subjects in most cases are theoretical, deliberately abstract with no emphasis on practice in related occupations. In Europe it is also virtually impossible (and at the very best universities unthinkable) to seek employment while at a university. Training to be gentlemen is the only task deemed appropriate to gentlemen's sons as well as those of tradesmen.

Flexible Programs, Credit System. The practice of varying study patterns so that they may be virtually tailor-made is also severely restricted in Europe and in the USSR and Japan. Immediate professional specialization in one faculty is the rule. Students train as lawyers, or doctors, or future professors, and programs are prescribed in detail—in the case of the USSR actually printed as personal diaries—to be followed minutely by the students. North America stands alone in pioneering an altogether different method of accounting for university work. In the United States students have great flexibility in choosing subjects of study and the sequences of subjects followed. Most include a healthy dose of courses in "basics," without which they cannot go on to graduate work in even the least professional schools. It is unthinkable not to have some courses in history, or sociology, or literature, or science, as part of a career in teaching, or law, or medicine, or business. But students also take a variety of other courses which are "derived" rather than basic: creative writing or journalism instead of or in addition to literature, animal husbandry instead of zoology, physical education in addition to anatomy.

The famous or infamous point-credit system has established a national measure of equivalence unprecedented in other countries. Nobody can tell what subject matter an individual student has covered without actually consulting his transcript. But the fact that he has accumulated 120 credit points suggests that he has attended an institution of higher education and followed courses appropriate to the first degree of bachelor of arts or sciences. A fairly standardized grading system also allows a tentative evaluation of performance level. A grading scale of five points (A to F) in undergraduate work and three points (A, B, and F) in graduate work allows the computation of cumulative grade averages. Honors for good progress such as being on the dean's list and graduation honors (summa or magna cum laude) mark the highpoints of this system in a manner suggesting the first-, second-, and third-class honors of English universities. Additional flexibility is provided through the "incomplete" grade. A student unable to finish course requirements in time can be granted one additional year to fulfill his class work. Increasingly also students are permitted to register for a simple pass/fail grade.

The American credit system has been much frowned on by European academicians, and they have profoundly criticized its lack of theoretical justification. Who can equate immersion in Plato with the study of calculus or, worse, with a course on preparation of morticians by assigning each a three-point credit value. But the somewhat clumsy system, the first valid attempt to establish automatic equivalence, permits the wide choices in shaping individual university careers. In Europe, Britain, France, and Sweden have begun experimenting in this direction.

Unregulated Studies. American and Canadian higher education also score higher marks than any other country in providing regular opportunities for interrupted studies. These consist of facilities for evening courses, opportunities for older people to return to university studies, sanction for interrupting study courses to travel abroad, or parallel studies at different universities. The practice of studying at different universities and thus accumulating credits for a degree at the parent institution is new in America but has an ancient tradition in Germany. The difference between American and European practices is not in kind but in degree.

There is in the United States and Canada a general readiness to accept unusual forms of study. This condition is partly due to the widespread feeling that the interests of individuals take precedence over the interests of the community. The universities, because they are either responsible to private boards of trustees or to public legislatures, are unusually nervous about public pressure and adverse opinions. Several unpublished case studies submitted to OECD by Earl McGrath document the willingness of American higher education institutions to adapt themselves to or even forestall the demands likely to be made on them. The pioneering and often unorthodox spirit of the United States is manifest in higher education. Nowhere else is there a University of the Seven Seas, a floating university on board a cruising ocean liner maintained by Chapman College, a rather small California institution. And Empire State College in New York will soon grant degrees for unorthodox and completely individualized programs or experiences.

In Europe most of the "spectacular" innovations are small in terms of numbers of students reached, and many peter out after their initial impulse is spent. American education, on the contrary, quite consciously uses novelty as a vehicle to provide excitement, to break down boredom and monopoly, and thus to keep education sparkling. This very attitude that "change is normal," as well as the great variety in curricular schemes appearing as a result, sets the USA apart as a highly innovative country. Recently Canada has begun rapidly to move in that direction too. The presence of a vast, articulate mass in the colleges has something to do with what is offered as programs. North American higher education, like its life in general, is for good or ill significantly moulded not by its leaders but by its participants. The notion invented here that one should dignify middle-level skills by providing them with the substance and prestige of college education is proving increasingly influential in the burgeoning higher education systems of Japan, the USSR, and Europe.

ACADEMIC FREEDOM
AND
PUBLIC CONTROL

7

While the universities attempt to solve their difficulties, the public stands outside the walls. Many want to enter and when refused want to know the reason. Many do enter and form opinions on what the universities ought to do, a matter which would have concerned them little in the earlier age of esoteric elitism. The massing of people has changed the cost picture until public taxation without representation is becoming an important issue. Society is tempted to interfere on behalf of progress when it discovers university professors to be too conservative, even more when it finds them too radical. In all, in our time the independence and self-government of the universities are seriously challenged. Though there is little doubt that they will be able to weather the storm, the redefinition of academic freedom in transnational terms seems inevitable in order to reconcile political differences as well as the differential impact of enrollments.

Mass higher education countries include those with capitalist and communist regimes. In both, industrialization and mass enrollment have been accompanied by increased demands for public participation, particularly in the administration of universities. In all countries problems of control are complicated by the fact that organization of tertiary education has become fragmented and pluralistic. In the Soviet Union the picture is the least diversified. With the exception of the Patrice Lumumba University of the Friendship of the Peoples, a special institution catering primarily to foreign students and financed indirectly by the state through special organizations, all other institutions are directly administered and financed by government. Until 1959, with the exception of the Ukraine this control was on the federal level. The inclusion of technicums within the jurisdiction of the Ministry of Higher Education has permitted some delegation of powers to the state level, through the creation of Ministries of Higher Education in each constituent republic. The work of faculty councils and academic senates permit some exercise of traditional faculty influence, even though financing, programs, and granting of degrees are reserved to the Ministry. But secondary coordination and control by the Party which the Soviets impose on all formal organizations is said also to operate in the universities. Japanese, Canadian, and US universities must coordinate the work of their universities through more complicated machinery. Japan alone has a Ministry of Education, a luxury denied the North Americans. All three countries must deal with federal or national and state or provincial or prefectural universities, or even with universities established and run by municipalities. Private universities further complicate the issue. In the USA extensively and in Japan partly, privately endowed universities have acquired considerable power through training national elites. In all three countries faculties have been more or less completely protected by law and custom from interference by the community in their affairs.

Once more Europe is in a different position. England is the only exception to the ministerial pattern of control, since it channels funds from the Treasury through a professor-dominated University Grants Committee. University government in all other European countries comes close to Japanese and Soviet patterns, which were modeled on Europe. Though the universities are thus dependent, the prestige and independence of faculties, though varying from country to country, are considerable. One needs to distinguish between issues of academic freedom and those dealing with pressure for increased control over universities. The latter pressure increases as the mass intake increases; the former is tied less to size than to political system. Only time can tell to what degree academic freedom will be modified by "massification," but geographical variations already in existence require us to anticipate new definitions.

Mounting Public Pressures

Internal turmoils in the university immediately register on the delicate seismograph of the watchful society. In the old days when universities were few and catered to the few who devoted themselves to contemplation, the universities could be aloof and left alone. Like cathedrals or palaces or the coliseum, they were ornamental parts of society, on the periphery of struggle for survival and power. Even then, as the early history of *cessatia* (suspension of lectures) and town-and-gown struggles testifies, being left alone was not easily accomplished. The loyal addresses which Oxford gave to each successive ruler, as the Stuarts were succeeded by Cromwell, by returning Stuarts, by William of Orange, and by the Hanoverians, are a mute, though not too edifying testimonial to outside pressures under which the universities labored.

At present, possessed of a fantastic influence everywhere, the university cannot escape interest if not outright invigilation on the part of the community. In an intensely politicized world the process of shaping leaders' ideas comes under constant scrutiny and suspicion. The university is like a car in a traffic jam. It cannot move back without declaring its indifference to political education. It cannot move forward to offer programs without incurring a charge from conservatives that it is too liberal and from liberals that it is too conservative. Even in a mass age the university must train managers, and every mismanagement may be laid on its doorstep by those who complain of miseducation.

The economic vista is equally clouded. The universities are by nature slow-movers, but they are asked to train people for a bewildering variety of professions in a rapidly changing market. People say "the future will be so complex, you cannot even imagine it." And then they say "the universities should prepare youth for it." If it cannot be imagined, it cannot be prepared for. In the future, training in specific skills may be taken over by specific on-the-job preparatory courses while the universities return to their time-honored function of imparting the irreducible minimum. It is their departure from *culture generale*, the *algemeine Bildung*, the *obshchee obrazovanie* that is so pointedly deplored when professors are accused of no longer being "renaissance."

Meanwhile, there are few signs, if any, of a return to such simplicity. While university faculties are chastized for not producing "the great integrators," society also pushes them inexorably to offer increasingly intricate specializations. The wider the extension of this process, the costlier the operation. In the present financial squeeze, American private universities have a hard time surviving in the open market. At Columbia University, for instance, student fees could meet the expenses of teaching departments, but the giant superstructure of computers, laboratories, libraries, and the hundreds of administrators and clerks employed to run the various services cannot be sustained except by grants and endowments. Necessity thus forces private universities into careful stances, building good public relations and high alumni support, careful planning, frugal husbandry of resources. Many an American university, to cite a familiar example, has wooed alumni by appealing to their alma mater spirit with impressive athletic teams, hoping that donations for stadiums and athletic scholarships will have leftovers for laboratories and libraries.

Though most of the world's universities are no longer of the private type, drawing sustenance from public funds supervised by public servants, the problems remain the same. The courting of regents on state boards, accountants on treasury committees, or ministerial officials alters only in degree, not in kind, the relationships the university must maintain. Public relations, planning, and financing are the major ingredients of university operation. Many academics think it a pity that these urgencies have crowded "ideas" out of so many heads involved in the task of keeping together the scholarly community.

The enrollment bulge in industrial countries has turned the universities into large-scale corporations. In the Soviet Union and Japan the effect is simply to increase the power of the administrative bureaucracies. In the USSR this power derives from a political elite, in Japan from a traditional elite. Soviet bureaucracy draws recruits substantially from the lower middle and lower classes but it nevertheless exhibits behaviors that are essentially conservative. The Japanese ruling circles until recently received men less freely from outside the traditional classes but their bureaucratic behavior has been essentially reformist. Despite these differences, in both countries university professors have to face governing groups that regard them quite simply as tools of national policy. North American and Western European countries assign universities somewhat more complicated roles. In the USA, Canada, and England even the state-financed universities are treated as having a somewhat mystic, extralegal existence. This cultural autonomy also stands out clearly in France, where its existence is acknowledged in spite of a routinized administrative system no different from that of Japan or the USSR. But even in these latter countries, in which decisions about where to build or how to develop tertiary education are centrally determined, there is an undefinable difference between the treatment of professors and that of other professionals. The concept of academic freedom, the orthodox cornerstone of the life of the universities and not that of actual control, still defines the relationship of the universities to the surrounding and supporting societies.

Academic Freedom and Survival

This concept requires redefinition under the impact of massification. The mission of a university involves an increasing number of functions: it owes service to the macrocosm of the world and the microcosm of its immediate neighborhood. These duties impinge on what is central to its being, the duty to make continued breakthroughs in knowledge. Under the orthodox notion of the university this centrality is jealously guarded; the academic community reacts with no little impatience to the harassment of outside obligations. But under the impact of new social forces the university has to defend its internal freedom to decide matters of teaching and research, and it is threatened even more imminently with loss of the external freedom to be involved or not involved in the concerns of society.

The political dependence of universities in some mass education countries is the extreme illustration of how the university position in society is changing. Educational experience outside the free context of the West suggests that the concept of academic freedom as a global principle needs to be broadened (see Bereday, 1967). Differentiated criteria of academic freedom and university autonomy are being debated to find ways in which universities in countries that refuse to act or cannot act fully in terms of a Western conception of *Lehrfreiheit* can still preserve what is essential in that tradition. Institutions of higher learning in many countries strive to live up to their obligation to further research, to teach, and to perform ancillary services in spite of severely circumscribed freedom as Western tradition understands it. Thus, the International Christian University in Tokyo demands as a condition of faculty appointment that the applicant be a Christian. Soviet universities apparently have a measure of academic effectiveness, even though the government emphasizes its right to total interference. Non-Communists have been flagrantly dismissed from universities in the USSR and Communists from US universities, and somehow these universities have carried on. In some cases, these infringements are exceptions to a general observance of academic freedom; in others they are more widespread.

Many countries live for periods of time under political tyranny, and their universities are forced to accommodate it. Custom rather than statute permits some tolerable degree of academic freedom to survive in adverse circumstances. Professors enduring authoritarian regimes have considerably more independence of action, especially in politically insensitive areas, than their governments would like to see. In sensitive areas, they are forced to dissemble by agreeing with the powers that be. When they are goaded into protests, they may lose their jobs or in some cases their lives. But such martyrdom of some may strengthen the dignity of others, and so long as that dignity is preserved, academic freedom is served even by breach and death. There is something unconquerable in the process of discussing great ideas with the young which keeps reasserting itself not only in spite of but because of persecution. Tyrants come and go, but universities as universities go on. No government has so far succeeded in discontinuing a university. The victory in the long run, even in countries with overpowering administrations, lies with those who persist in seeking independence even while under the yoke of oppression.

Breaches of academic freedom in non-Western universities

are more calamitous than in the West, but only in degree. The Western tradition itself has been blighted by some fairly serious corrosions. One is forced to differentiate academic freedom from university autonomy. The former has, on the whole, been preserved in statute and custom while the latter has historically been limited by various agencies of society. Certainly, moving away from the academic self-government which still survives in considerable measure at Oxford and Cambridge, the universities have accepted the control of bureaucratic, financial, or religious circles, and lately even of students.

But the distinction between university autonomy and academic freedom, though useful, really is part of a continuum. The freedom of individuals cumulatively adds up to the autonomy of all. If the autonomy of all is limited by statute, then safeguarding it by custom alone is bound to break down at crucial moments for all. Ashby (1956) defines collective freedom as a flow of academic business upward from departments to the senate. But he also remarks that, whatever flows upward, money (and hence control) is sure to flow downward. An autocratic university administration even in a free country like the United States (particularly in small institutions where professors are not distinguished enough to be irreplaceable) can stifle the substance even though leaving intact the outward forms of academic freedom. University independence is highly treasured in the West, but it is also marred in practice by imperfections. Most universities strive for freedom; few prossess it absolutely. The question, therefore, is where does "unfreedom" end and freedom begin?

From the experience of mass higher education countries emerges a definition of academic freedom and university autonomy based on a minimum rather than a maximum standard, which allows faculties to salvage elements of freedom in a large setting of unfreedom. Several components make up this definition.

First, individual freedom and collective autonomy of university faculties may be said to be encouraged where the machinery of appointment and dismissal, of whatever kind, does not bring in professors incompetent to teach their specialty. This criterion means that the university's role as a place of learning and of free inquiry is not completely eclipsed if a set of protesting professors is replaced by an alternative but equally educationally effective set of consenting professors who, whatever their political attitudes, succeed in maintaining a high tradition of research and teaching. Where, however, a purge causes the replacement of staff members by a group of untrained or semitrained persons distinguished only by appropriate political credentials, or where the infringement of academic freedom demoralizes those who remain so that they cannot operate effectively, we may say that academic freedom has been deeply damaged.

Second, academic freedom and university autonomy may be said to be maintained whenever some form of statutory or customary "due process" is preserved in dealing with university affairs. The record of recent disputes between the university and society includes many instances of refusal of promotion or dismissal, which, though infringements of custom, were not really breaches of academic freedom since statutory process was not infringed. Unfortunately the record also contains many cases of peremptory appointment by the government or dismissal or even kidnapping obviously outside due process and, therefore, violations of academic statute. By and large the process which protects faculty immunities is legally defined in most countries, certainly in all industrial countries. Where there is no such definition, a university may be said to have ceased to exist.

Third, freedom in the university promises to be maintained if there is in being a community of scholars whose collective opinion is an active force in university life, specifically in determining the rewards and punishments of its members. Even under quite severe limitations of autonomy, some academic freedom exists if members' academic conduct is guided by the pressure of their colleagues' professional, scholarly, and scientific opinions. It is the academic community that determines the competence of its members and by its acceptance sanctions those statutes and customs that constitute the due process of its government. Violations of academic freedom may wound the community, but as long as it can rally and resume academic life, the university continues. Under this broad definition, South African universities have survived the shock of racial policies and of the dismissals resulting from them. Other universities continue to chart their course in spite of intrusions by party or state. In all these cases a consensus of the academic community to get on with university life in spite of violations is the crucial point. The moral and intellectual staying power of professors is the product of their collective judgment of whether or not minimum conditions for continuing academic life have been preserved.

Extramural Impact

These new definitions pinpoint the current level of outside interference with the internal life of the universities. But what about the reverse—the impact universities make when interacting with and influencing outside society?

University connections with national bodies are almost automatic. In most countries university graduates occupy all important positions, and university professors act as consultants to government if not as *the* government. Professors seldom lead their countries directly, as was the case in the USA under Wilson, in Portugal under Salazar, and very often in Italy. But in the United States, at least since the New Deal, and certainly since the Kennedy administration, professors figure most visibly as persons of trust in important national responsibilities. In the USSR, as also in Japan and Canada, there is a more visible separation between academic and governing groups, yet in these countries also the government relies heavily on the cooperation and advice of professional bodies. In the Soviet Union the Academy of Sciences is the chief instrument for formulating the party line in matters of culture and science as is the Academy of Pedagogical Sciences in education. In Japan the various national advisory councils are similarly staffed with academicians. The National Institute of Educational Research (*Kokuritsu Kiyoiku Kenkiujo*) is the academic body of the Ministry of Education, while the more direct Research Section (*Chosaka*) is handled by civil servants. In Canada recent higher education reforms have been formulated by committees heavily manned by professors. While in France *les mandarins* exercise a quasi-dictatorial influence over national culture, in Germany professors are civil servants, virtually interchangeable with the *Ministerialrat* and eagerly sought as members of "advisory boards or as assembly speakers by all types of organizations, from political parties to interior decorators" (Boning and Roeloff, 1969, p. 120). In spite of pressures and hostilities felt by the universities the penetration of the power structure by professors as consultants is everywhere so substantial as to warrant little further innovation.

Less felicitous is contact between universities and local communities, and better coordination needs to be effected. Since early town-and-gown disputes, the universities have had to establish their independence not only from local burghers who claimed jurisdiction but also from bishops and crown ministers with similar convictions. The defensive stance of the universities as corporate organizations was further complicated at the local level when faculties began identifying with high social class and with the national and international instead of the local scene. Tensions inherent in the development of local cooperation are described elegantly and at length in Perkin's discerning study on establishment of the new universities in the United Kingdom. In each case "enormous goodwill" at first prevailed as high expectations of local citizens for enhanced prestige were combined with their new cultural aspirations. Swiftly there followed disenchantment, primarily because of the "supposed arrogance of many of the university staff in not taking a (preferably supplicant and subordinate) place in the hierarchy of social life, in the round of cocktail and dinner parties, in the Rotary Club, Masonic Lodge, golf and country clubs" (1969, p. 211).

Expanding universities in all countries run into some such problems. Different cultural interests, different life styles and aspirations of college faculties and local citizens are common all over the world and settled everywhere, at best, in an uneasy truce. Recent innovations try to smooth such collaboration. At the University of Lancaster in England a Town and Gown Club has been set up by the vice-chancellor and the town clerk, not only as a forum of polite social contact but for the airing of controversies (Perkin, 1969, p. 215). In Germany both at Bochum and Konstanz, Societies of Friends of the University were established, composed of leading local personalities. In Yugoslavia Educational Associations have been set up by law to act as links between educational and community activities. Still in the initial stages of operation, these associations, charged also with financing duties, nonetheless "remained fairly closed bodies whose contact with citizen and interested organizations were not always very strong." On the whole, efforts aimed at local contact and cooperation have not as yet improved substantially with massification. In contrast with Soviet lower schools, where parent committees are quite active, the VUZY (higher schools) remain fairly isolated from the public. In Japan, outside the municipal universities, there is also little contact between university and community. In the USA and Canada wealthy donors are often responsible for buildings and scholarships, but these acts even in urban universities lack the force of the Parent-Teacher Associations. Perhaps the weakness of these efforts is evidenced by the surprise one feels that they were made at all. At least they show that universities are beginning to feel some obligation toward local people.

The most important instrument of university involvement is continuing education or extension activities. These efforts are more natural indices of university interest, because after all academics may be expected to respond more easily to a call for intellectual service than to the display of social courtesies. But here, too, the stance of the universities is uncertain and varies from place to place. This variation derives from the two educational traditions behind the postsecondary education of persons who are not full-time students at the university or equivalent institutions (see Bereday, 1973).

The first tradition, more substantial historically, is continuing education, whose roots are in adult education and outside the universities. Its premise is that it is desirable for human beings to take refresher courses, to be retrained for new or changing job specifications, and to pursue constructive hobbies. Such education, it is said, should be spontaneous, ad hoc, in direct response to need, untrammeled by rules and regulations common in higher education. This type of education should also be of mass character, accessible to all without previous qualifications. We are likely to hear about continuation much more, now that proposals for education "from cradle to grave" are increasingly being put forward.

The second position is that continuing education should be part of university services. This educational position is based on the conviction that it is the business of the university to serve the masses, that its certifying function should be used when appropriate to legitimize cultural activities beyond its walls, that the residential, full-time, day character of most universities is incidental, a matter of traditional style. If the true function of universities is to guard the levels of knowledge transmitted, then flexible imaginative exercise of this guardianship, it is argued, should include a "third function" of community services, in addition to the traditional teaching and research.

It is not easy or perhaps even fruitful to assign priority to these contentions. We can be certain that continuing education will burgeon. We shall have more of the kind of vocational courses from furniture-finishing to photography now offered in, say, Boston or Cambridge adult education centers. Demand will continue also for philosophy or literature as dispensed by Danish Folk High Schools or the Workers Education Association in England. When such courses are similar to what higher education offers, increasing demands will be made for university recognition. Even when they diverge from traditional subjects, as in the case of shorthand or motor mechanics, pressure will be brought to bear via the polytechnic movement to find a place for them within the academic sanctuary. Some universities may for a time resist such intrusions with varying degrees of success, but it is doubtful that they can stem the tide. Successful resistance could happen only in the unlikely event that the mass education themes now spreading are ultimately rebuffed by those who favor the older elite system.

At the same time one can speculate that extension education in the universities may even put itself out of business by its own action. When performance reaches high levels, extension courses will naturally be identified with the internal curriculum and eventually become part of it. Internal and external courses may merge to form a complete system of continuing education, with courses being offered both on campus and off campus, or extension courses may cease to exist because continuation is only one minor phase of the mass education movement. The major phase, regular day and evening classes on campus, is expanding vigorously. Also, new universities are proliferating in remote places where in the past only extension courses flourished. As more people have a chance to take regular courses, the demand for extension courses may correspondingly decrease.

Clearly, we can no longer speak of a simple dichotomy between nonuniversity- and university-sponsored continuing education. A comparative overview reveals three stages: nonacademic, semiacademic, and academic, or nonuniversity continuation, university-sponsored extramural courses, and autonomous off-campus university extension.

All countries have networks of continuing education unrelated to universities. Libraries and museums are, of course, everywhere. Youth study classes established by the Japanese government are matched by courses established by business companies in Germany and professional organizations in the USSR. Similar ones are being developed in Britain, Canada, and other countries. The titles of a series of books by Clark and Sloan describe the American situation. *Classrooms in the Factories, Classrooms in the Stores, . . . in the Military, . . . in Camps, . . . in the Main Street* suggest a vast network of out-of-school education. The last-mentioned book claims that there exist in the United States several thousand schools whose identity can only be uncovered by consulting the yellow pages of the telephone book. Dropouts from public schools are dropins to the vast array of educational facilities. Systems of education by radio as in Colombia or by television as in Italy have also been established outside the universities. Sometimes, as in the case of Ruskin College at Oxford, continuing education nestles right in the midst of a university town under the shadow of the university but has refused or been refused admittance.

At the other end of the scale is off-campus education completely incorporated in the university structure. This type is found particularly in Canada and other countries of British tradition. As full-time resources become scarce the demand for extension education is given more weight. The External Department of the University of London reaches around the world. The School of General Studies at Columbia University more modestly serves adults locally. At the University of Queensland, the Department of External Education and the relevant Board of Studies dated from 1949. In New Zealand the creation of Massay University in 1969 brought within the structure the correspondence courses of an older 1960 institution. The University of the Air scheduled to begin operations in Tokyo is affiliated with other Japanese universities. The boldest innovation is the British Open University, which is totally independent, the first noncampus university. But even there, "ground" courses as against television courses have recently been increasing. Complete merger between internal and external studies has not yet been accomplished, but appointing a distinguished academic as head of the external division, forcing internal faculty to teach also externally, and insisting on strict identity of the content of courses are the standard demands of reformers anxious for complete integration. When this is successful, as in Queensland, course outlines prepared for external use may be in much demand from internal students. Correspondence study in New Zealand is not open to students who live within commuting distance from the university and who apparently might prefer it. Soviet correspondence courses require students to be bodily present in the sponsoring university at the beginning and end of the school year. Differences in prestige between full-time and correspondence courses are said to be small in the USSR. Little can be said about the long-range effects of a thoroughly "merged" university system since all known fusions are recent and, with the growth of mass education, may prove impermanent. But the efforts of the pioneering countries must be watched with interest as test cases.

Between the polarities of nonuniversity education for adults and fully autonomous correspondence departments in the universities we find a great variety of provisions for partial union of extramural studies with on-campus work. These provisions illustrate how efforts to bridge the gap between nonuniversity adult education and off-campus university education are currently pursued. Extension units are a common feature of North American and English universities though they are seldom full-fledged academic departments. In contrast, the evening department at Birbeck College at the University of London has achieved an integral status. Traveling lecturers, tutoring by correspondence, distributing study outlines and books, part-time "sandwich" attendance, weekend seminars—these are some standard features of university-affiliated extension courses. Television lectures and lectures by telephone have now been added to the repertoire.

Extramural education in this middle position is still an academic Cinderella. Not all and sometimes no credits earned in this way are accepted for internal degrees. External and part-time units are plagued by high drop-out rates, less thorough preparation of instruction, and sometimes inexperienced lecturers. Often the popularity of the subjects offered has little to do with the quality of programs. Sometimes changes outside the system, such as modifications in the requirements for teachers' certificates, mean alterations in the demand for certain subjects. (This particular change is especially important because teachers tend to be the best customers for correspondence work.) Since students tend to migrate toward large cities, some dropouts from extension courses may switch to on-campus studies.

The major trend visible at present is a shift along the continuum: from continuation education to partial union with the university (the state of concubinage) to a proper marriage. To control this change policy bodies and planning councils are beginning to emerge. Some have been hostile to the shift but were overruled by the authorities. Others, such as the Japanese Council for Social Education, have urged the government to effect a closer union, even by giving subsidies. Yet another body, the British Council for National Academic Awards (CNAA), was created to legitimize non-university higher degrees, although by so doing it has weakened the chances that colleges which prepare for these degrees will merge with universities.

Awareness of the continuing education or extension problem has grown remarkably throughout the world. But in practice only small inroads have been made into the world of the universities. Here and there, brilliant new projects are proposed and experimented with, but comparative overview reveals continuing variations in level of academic advancement and in planning and execution. At the end of the road to merger lie more discomforts. As colleges of education or of social work have found out, even complete inclusion in the university has not saved them from the inferiority of being assigned to the lowest ranks of the academic pecking order.

The ambitions of extension education, however, are part of the wide assault on the universities. Their main weapon is the assertion that the community has a duty to bring maximum knowledge right to the individual's doorstep. The universities are under pressure to admit the validity of that proposition. If and when they do, extension education will have done its part to revise the traditional concepts of higher education.

Independence Within Dependence

It would be a calamity for human civilization if the universities were to disappear. To have lived and worked within one is to know the difference between wisdom and cleverness, uprightness and false fronts, truth and mendacity. No learned society, no convent, no political cabinet can match, let alone outdo, the indefinable magnetism present on university campuses. Only in that human institution has the loftiest of all human maxims—"To thy own self be true"—come anywhere near to fruition. Only through the perennial conversation between resident masters immersed in reflection and future young leaders earning their spurs in the lecture rooms can accumulated human knowledge be kept fresh and readily available for use.

All these qualities of university life continue to shine through in mass countries, in spite of continuous deviations and abuses. If an argument can be at all sustained that the substance of university life is capable of popularization without vulgarization, nothing short of universal implementation will do to fulfill man's relentless quest for ennoblement. Such a proposition commits higher education to close contact with the world outside its walls, and the greatest inspiration and beauty the universities can provide to the community is in handling the various pressures of society in a just manner (see Bereday, 1956).

In the universities, which are explicitly the centers of free thought, the schools of critical thinking, and the carriers of enlightenment, the problem of academic courage more than of freedom must be central. The universities are now subject to criticism. In the soul-searching process of reviewing its institutions, society cannot fail to scrutinize its higher learning. Intellectual arrogance is the cause of a steady murmur that the universities do not live up to their mission, that they have tried to offer leadership instead of guidance, dictation instead of inspiration, doctrinaire certitude and sarcasm instead of scholarly humility and caution. Much defense of the universities has been of the finest quality. But some defenders of academic freedom in North America, Europe, or Japan have defined it as the denial of society's right to criticize. Outside pressures on the universities as in USSR were feared as likely to stifle free thought. Teachers were deemed so vulnerable to attack that they might cease to be heard altogether once an attempt was made to repress them. In the interest of academic freedom, it was said, the universities ought to be left alone by society to carry on their business.

But an increasing number of societies have come to feel that the universities, though independent, must not be regarded as isolated bastions of learning which have a monopoly on preserving and interpreting culture. All universities are chartered organizations to which certain functions have been entrusted by society. Society suffers the teachers, and those in countless other occupations, to withhold their hands from the actual business of production because it wishes to receive services in other areas. The furthering of intellectual discoveries, the perpetuation of culture, the guardianship of its values, the education of its young, and above all the display of social courage: these are the undisputed tasks of the universities.

University professors are chosen to carry out these tasks, but it is now felt that these tasks are not given to them as in irrevocable trust for the management of which they are answerable to God alone. The democratic society, whose very essence is the system of checks and balances, in government by public ventilation of grievances and by corporate discussion, has the right and indeed the obligation to hold professors responsible and to call them to account for the fulfillment of these tasks. Because of their lofty functions, the corporate life of the universities and the individual lives of their professors must at all times be open to full public scrutiny. Only if upon examination they are continually found to be above reproach can the universities fulfill their goal of teaching generation after generation to live nobly, beautifully, and freely.

Professors are not, in this view, damaged by outside controls. A life of beauty, nobility, and freedom must not only be taught; it must be lived, and if need be, fought for. Criticism and repressions must not be lamented. They must be faced. Explanations must be given, errors must be admitted, opinions must be clarified and reaffirmed, and convictions must be defended. Some critics ask professors to be aware that if criticism comes unjustly, society's injustice is that of the alumni, a painful remainder of the educational failure of previous generations of professors. The universities ought to follow Matthew Arnold in believing that freedom to speak means not only the right to say what one thinks but also the duty to keep silent unless one has something worth saying.

Cowardice, in spite of much recent shame, is not in fact the true historical record of the teaching profession. Medieval teachers suspended lectures or migrated if thwarted by other agencies of society. Certainly Cambridge grew from Oxford in this way. More recently, Harvard quietly but firmly disregarded attacks by Senator McCarthy on its integrity. Could it be that its stand somehow released other hitherto timid agencies of the American community to defend themselves from similar accusations in the months following? While obviously prefering total cultural and political autonomy, professors in mass countries have been resigned enough to accommodate the new specifications. The fear of losing funds or jobs is ultimately not a perfect silencer of academic men. University freedom is a living ideal and not a mere cliche, and professors have learned what it means to be attacked and even to be investigated. By definition their universities are the battlegrounds of ideas. Our time has shown that when professors find themselves in the universities which have lost pride in free thought, they seek new universities at which freedom can continue to flourish.

Universities in country after country are realizing that the true meaning of academic freedom lies not in avoiding pressure but in defying it when it comes. The strength of free man is to challenge inquiry and criticism, not to shudder before it. When professors are silenced by attacks made on them, the universities have ceased to perform the function which was entrusted to them by society. Those who demand immunity from criticism on the ground that it will silence the professors surely furnish the best proof that the profession has so declined as to deserve to be criticized.

Those who uphold freedom to think and to speak are not really vulnerable to attack if they are prepared to be missionaries. There is only one freedom of thought, not several kinds, and that freedom, if it is to impress anyone in a mass age, must be a forceful, living thing practiced by the whole profession, not just by a few courageous people. Professors, the intellectual elite of the world,

more than any other group, have often displayed the courage born
of devotion to freedom. The defiant challenge, not helpless cower-
ing behind the walls of academic immunities; pride in freedom, not
fear for security; honor more than tenure; staunch, powerful living:
these as displayed throughout traditional history and now in the
recent history of massification are the surest guarantees that the universities will continue to be bastions of freedom.

TOWARD A THEORY
OF MASS
HIGHER EDUCATION

8

Much has changed in the universities of industrial countries since that fateful day on the eve of World War I when an English statesman was moved to say that the lights were going out all over Europe and would not be seen in his lifetime again. All over the world the lights came on again twice, and a peaceful future in freedom is at least a possibility. But mankind must face the realistic implementation of the very ideals with which Europe has successfully injected so many other continents.

One basic truth needs to be realized at the outset when approaching the prognosis of higher education in a mass age. It is an extremely general truth, almost trite, always crucial. Most countries outside the industrial belt of the USA, Western Europe, the USSR, and Japan are confronted with one fundamental problem—physical *hunger*. In spite of industrialization, half of the world's population will go to bed hungry tonight. Of children born today, one quarter has no chance of ever learning how to read and write, the skills without which they cannot take steps to better their condition. Though the upper reaches of education systems in all countries, rich or poor, resemble each other in their intellectual performance and social urbanities, this resemblance conceals the basic fact that outside the industrial countries those elevated university systems rest on a destitute population.

In rich industrial countries these hungry masses are looked upon sometimes with horror and sometimes with fear. Not only is there chagrin and shock over all the inhumanity and ignorance, but these masses are seen as a potential danger, prone to communism or at least to anger and revolution. But alas the hungry, as the last thousand years of our history plainly show, far from being explosive, are born to obedience. A hungry man can be rendered a slave for a piece of bread and for a cake he can be made to lick the boots of his master. Once the hunger is removed, once the fear of it is phased out as the basic factor of motivation, men are free to desire a new, more human quality. Men who have bread desire *dignity*.

Whatever the future may hold "beyond freedom and dignity," we would do well to view the entire last century of educational efforts in industrial countries not so much as a search for bread but as a search for dignity. Bread in the northern belt is available to everyone through work in an open or collective market, through organized effort in trade unions, through welfare, through electoral pressure in democracies, and through public opinion pressure in controlled systems. If all else fails, in rare cases bread could be demanded through violent means, through riots and demonstrations. Fear of such eruptions rather than they themselves has abolished the remaining hunger in mass societies.

The residuum of human desires is for self-respect and dignity, and this thousandfold motivation pours itself into education. One can "play games" of organizing schools and especially their crown, the schools of higher education, "thus or thus." But nothing that ignores man's quest for dignity is likely to last. It is a natural instinct for the encephalizing man to treasure and to reach toward the ideal of wisdom. But the minute a group of wise men organize themselves to shut the gate in the face of other men's quest, they leave beyond the walls not acquiescence but rage. The elitist universities which still survive in mass countries, mothballed with memories of the not-too-distant age in which they, too, presided over hungry nations, often do not want to accept this fact. Instead, mere palliatives are offered to the angry surge of educational ambitions of the mass. The fatuous hope is that these halfhearted gestures may somehow stem the tide. Thus the very wisdom for the protection of which the universities federated themselves and for which they should be admired is put to question. Rigor, maturity, serenity are what the university represents to those who have known it at its best from inside. Hypocrisy, snobbishness, and mendacity are what it appears to be to the disappointed millions all around.

It will not do to accuse the masses of seeking higher education to gain the lucrative economic rewards that were for long associated with distinguished professional, university-derived status. During the week these words were written policemen and firemen in New York City demanded and received new contracts granting them an annual salary of fifteen thousand dollars. In the very same week several able applicants were denied consideration for twelve-thousand-dollar assistant professorships at Columbia, even though they had completed their work for the Ph.D. What is sought is not money but dignity derived from high professional position. In an industrial society there is simply no avoiding the social significance of educational aspirations.

During recent decades the universities of industrial countries have gone through a remarkable period of expansion. They have responded to that expansion with a level of innovation which is on the whole insignificant. After years of assault on the structure through which men at the top control the flow of talent from below, most of the familiar features of university government remain intact and youth, whether young teachers or students, remain for the most part in tutelary positions. Curriculum varies across the nations, but even in the new universities there are few bright islands of freshness. New universities and new programs in the old institutions tend in time to revert to traditional positions. The pressure for more university places is being, in part at least, successfully deflected into nonuniversity institutions not connected with the upper system. The heroic or pathetic efforts at education by the less able or poorer students, by people who work days and study nights, are short-changed by bestowal of largely third-rate qualifications. Anyone who has ever watched young persons crowding with fervor into physician's aids schools, secretarial schools, community colleges, and other similar institutions must sense that there is something wrong in rewarding so much effort with diplomas which do not have an appropriate intellectual value or social recognition.

But the actual level of innovations in higher education is not the central issue. Even if one-half or more of all youngsters entered college, nothing would be changed so long as they encountered an elitist frame of mind. People in search of dignity have always the choice of feeling "as good as most" or "better than most." As a rule Europeans and the others who share their university traditions prefer the latter position. Even egalitarians in Europe shock American egalitarians with the many unconscious ways they voice opinions that are subtly elitist. A thousand years of building and treasuring high-level intellectual fortresses have made such a deep impression that it is impossible to dismiss the sentries at the gate. As a result, though the drawbridge may no longer be always up, watchful hands are nervously on the lever. In contemplating change in higher education, elitist planners must first address themselves to their own psychological reservations.

Perhaps people can be made to feel unique rather than better than others. Too many are humiliated by being told of their inadequacy instead of being spurred to effort by being told of their potential. In an age in which our very life depends on machines, should there be so many differences between manual and mental talents? When instant retrieval of information is being assured by computers, must there be so much insistence on prerequisites and proper sequences? When knowledge is exploding those trained most recently know the most. Why, then, continue outmoded seniority systems as if length of experience meant wisdom rather than obsolescence? Most important, when all participate in political decisions or in the viewer culture created by national TV, what tragic error prompts some people in universities to regard them as upper-class clubs instead of palaces of national culture?

University planners need to adopt a new frame of mind, to solve problems of large admissions in positive ways instead of reinforcing methods of rejection. Then educational evidence will begin to flow into patterns and will allow a theory of mass education to emerge.

In reaching for that theory we can now say, first of all, that open admission can be charged only in a very short run with "lowering quality" (see Bereday, 1971a). In the long run education ennobles and improves comprehension. Open admission brings the vigor and ambitions of many into play. High standards are damaged by this massing of new human energy only when such standards are themselves pedantic and obsolete. Mass experiments in the USA, because it was a pioneer, have produced many lapses from grace alongside some outstanding successes. But the intellectual levels attained along with mass entry in Canada, Japan, and the USSR provide reasonable proof that quantity need not damage quality.

Second, arguments for open admission need no longer be linked to a consideration of how many highly educated people the economy can absorb. There is now no such thing as overproduction of men and women with high qualifications. A major though still too little recognized feature of mass societies is the educational upgrading of all occupations. High levels of education enable people in erstwhile low-level occupations to command better pay, to insist on cultured working conditions, and to give more enlighted service. John Gardner's often repeated phrase is worth repeating again: A country which values second-rate philosophers more than first-rate plumbers will find that neither its pipes nor its ideas hold water.

Third, the notion of mass education does not imply an egalitarian but an open school. Part of mass theory is the belief that all human beings are infinitely educable, and when they are not, the reasons are not innate but environmental and therefore curable. Heredity is in itself an accumulation of environments, and though the perfection of academic comprehension may not be totally possible in one generation, it can be steadily improved from parents to children across the generations.

Only thus far mass theory is egalitarian. This means that mass universities cannot remain elitist and cater only to the best, it also means that they must not cater to all in equal measures. Mass school is not egalitarian but compensatory. The curriculum must give most to those who have the least in order to increase the academic comprehension of the mass rather than simply reinforce already existing disparities. Higher education must now concentrate on motivating the average to high attainment rather than being content to hold up the able to high standards. The onus of reform in mass universities is to upgrade nonuniversity subjects not only to the *status* but to the *level* of university studies. The mass university is meant to ennoble a vocational interest in cooking by leading the learner from reading the menu to the French language, and from the use of pressure cookers to the theory of thermodynamics. It is supposed to turn an undertaker into a funeral counselor by coaxing him into studying the sociology of grief and metaphysics. When the University of Michigan is forced by black students to admit black candidates without being allowed to pass upon their credentials, implied in this apparent outrage is the recognition that in the act of selection the universities must not automatically enforce their own one-sided view of excellence. It is not a crime for even the stupid to seek high levels of education, and social customs which reject such aspirations can hardly be repositories of ultimate human wisdom.

Mass education so defined will probably evoke derisive laughter from many elitist readers; it raises the temperature of many within the mass education countries themselves. But throughout the last hundred years, over the din of constant lament, the scope of mass education has been relentlessly expanding. It cannot be licked, it must be joined. Those who cooperate have a chance to influence the trend with the wisdom of their own experience.

No one can be sure whether what is happening now in the universities of advanced countries is wisdom or aberration. Perhaps there is prudence in the European style of following warily in the footsteps of the cultures it created and of attempting to test the right mix between old serenities and future dynamics. But the only real argument can be about how controlled the growth should be—that there should be growth seems a foregone conclusion. Until and unless history is given the chance to evaluate the effects of mass intake into higher education we will never be permitted to study the lesson. The courageous, dynamic nations willing to take on their shoulders the pioneering risks of mass higher education have already demonstrated the compelling need for this most important human discovery.

It is crucial to make oneself believe that all men are infinitely educable, that potentially there is no limit to their capabilities. During thousands of years of intellectual labor, mankind has put forth in each century a few Einsteins or Schweitzers. Are there only a few in each age? Maybe at the end of the climb there lies a society of Einsteins and Schweitzers. We shall never know until we try. And even if this dream should prove false, the universities, all education, must act as if it were true. In education hope is the only stock-in-trade. A glass is never half empty, only half full. Hope is the only source of motivation. Destroy hope that hard effort in learning can be crowned by wisdom and you destroy the spine of education. The lesson for all nations, inexorably arising out of comparative evidence, is that they must move further and faster into the age of mass education.

BIBLIOGRAPHY

Several supporting materials from the Organization for Economic Cooperation and Development (OECD), some published, some in mimeographed form, were available to round off the sources for consultation. Of these the most directly relevant was a series of restricted documents reporting an inquiry by the OECD Directorate for Scientific Affairs entitled *Statistical Survey of Developments in Higher Education*. The survey, collected in 1968, consists of a general introduction, a comparative document on quantitative trends and country studies for Germany, Austria, Belgium, Canada, Denmark, Spain, the USA, France, Greece, Ireland, Italy, Luxembourg, Norway, Netherlands, Portugal, the United Kingdom, Sweden, Switzerland, Turkey, Japan, and Yugoslavia. The figures cover all types of institutions of higher education, broadly defined, and provide a full picture and projected growth of enrollments, admissions and graduations, and ratios of men to women and of students to age groups.

Another study by the Directorate of Scientific Affairs carried out in 1970 provides materials on educational growth. Data for Yugoslavia, Belgium, Greece, Denmark, Spain, Ireland, Italy, Norway, Holland, and Sweden were available. In these qualitative stud-

ies the governments concerned project their plans for educational
expansion, including innovations in higher education. In 1970 also,
the OECD Committee for Scientific and Technical Personnel held
a conference on Policies for Educational Growth. Several volumes—
Educational Growth Since 1950 (Vol. 1), *Teaching Personnel and
Expansion of Places* (Vol. 3), *Group Disparities in Participation*
(Vol. 4), *Educational Policies* (Vol. 5) and *Changes in Secondary
and Higher Education* (Vol. 6)—were available.

A very abundant third source dealt with teacher training.
Under this heading a series of mimeographed materials was prepared dealing with quantitative growth of the faculties in higher
education. A general report was accompanied by twenty-one country reports, which included, in addition to Western Europe, the
USA, Canada, and Japan. The other study of teacher education
included an extensive series by the Committee for Scientific and
Technical Personnel in 1969. One volume dealt in general with the
Supply and Demand for Primary and Secondary Teachers, another
much shorter with *Training, Recruitment and Utilization of Teachers* at the same level. Country reports backed this study, the first
volume dealing with France and Ireland, another with Germany,
Belgium, and Britain, the last with Spain, Iceland, Norway, and
Turkey as well as Canada, Japan, and the United States.

While the present book was being written, two further very
valuable OECD documents appeared. One, *Planning New Structures of Post-Secondary Education,* contains several country reports
as well as a discerning general paper on short-cycle higher education. The other, part of the *Reviews of National Policies for Education,* presents illuminating records of the confrontation meetings between Japan, Germany, and others and the OECD examiners.

Two sources by related international organizations were also
employed: a study by the Council for Cultural Cooperation of the
Council of Europe published in 1967 and entitled *Reform and Expansion of Higher Education in Europe* (reports by fourteen European countries about reforms in higher education in the previous
decade); reports from the Conference on University Reforms, held
in Ragaz in April 1970 under the auspices of the Institute of the
European Community for University Studies, which presented re-

forms qualitatively and dealt with Belgium, Germany, Britain, Switzerland, Sweden, Holland, Italy, and France.

Other sources of reference are listed alphabetically below.

ASHBY, E. "Self-Government in Modern Universities." *Science and Freedom,* Dec. 1956, *7,* 3–10.

BEN-DAVID, J. *Fundamental Research and the Universities.* Paris: OECD, n.d., 64.

BEREDAY, G. Z. F. "The Educational Background of Prominent Professional Men." *Pilot Papers,* 1947, *2*(4), 76–92.

BEREDAY, G. Z. F. "The Freedom to Attack the Universities." *Journal of Higher Education,* 1956, *27*(1), 8–10.

BEREDAY, G. Z. F. "Reflections on Comparative Methodology in Education." *Comparative Education,* 1967a, *3*(3), 169–187.

BEREDAY, G. Z. F. "Autonomy and Academic Freedom." *Minerva,* 1967b, *5*(7), 266–269.

BEREDAY, G. Z. F. "Selective Education versus Education for All." In E. K. Garber and J. M. Crossett (Eds.), *Liberal and Conservative; Issues for College Students.* Glenview, Ill.: Scott Foresman, 1968.

BEREDAY, G. Z. F. "School Systems and Mass Demand: A Comparative Overview." In G. Z. F. Bereday (Ed.), *Essays on World Education.* New York: Oxford University Press, 1969, pp. 93–110.

BEREDAY, G. Z. F. "Home Thoughts from Abroad: A Comparative View on Learning for the Masses." *The Times,* London, January 15, 1971a, p. 8.

BEREDAY, G. Z. F. "College and Non-College—the Changing Social Values of Education." In S. D. Kertesz (Ed.), *The Task of the Universities in a Changing World.* Notre Dame: University of Notre Dame Press, 1971b, pp. 111–122.

BEREDAY, G. Z. F. "Higher Education in Comparative Perspective." *The Annals of the American Academy of Political and Social Science,* Nov. 1972a, *404,* 21–30.

BEREDAY, G. Z. F. "Post-Compulsory not Post-Secondary; New Look at Upper Curriculum Patterns." *Journal of Abstracts in International Education,* Winter/Spring 1972b, *3,* 1–4.

BEREDAY, G. Z. F. "The Contribution of Comparative Education to Comparative Studies of Adult Education." *Journal of International Congress of University Adult Education*, May 1973.

BIGELOW, K. "The Passing of Teachers College." *Teachers College Record*, 1957, *58*(8), 409–417.

BONING, E., AND ROELOFF, K. *Innovation in Higher Education: Three German Universities, Aachen, Bochum, Konstanz.* Paris: OECD, 1970.

BOURDIEU, P., AND PASSERON, J. C. *La Reproduction.* Paris: Editions Minuit, 1970.

BURN, B. B. *Higher Education in Nine Countries: A Comparative Study of Colleges and Universities Abroad.* New York: McGraw-Hill, 1971.

BURGESS, T., AND PRATT, J. *Innovation in Higher Education: Technical Education in the United Kingdom.* Paris: OECD, 1971.

Carnegie Commission on Higher Education. *Less Time, More Options: Education Beyond the High School.* New York: McGraw-Hill, 1971.

Central Council for Education. *Interim Report on Fundamental Policies and Measures for the Overall Expansion and Development of School Education in the Future.* Tokyo: Ministry of Education, 1969.

CERYCH, L., AND FURTH, D. E. "On the Threshold of Mass Higher Education." In R. W. Niblett and R. F. Butts (Eds.), *Universities Facing the Future.* San Francisco: Jossey-Bass, 1972, pp. 14–28.

CURLE, A. "Education, Politics and Development." *Comparative Education Review*, Feb. 1964, *7*, 226–245.

DE VOS, G., AND WAGATUMA, H. *Japan's Invisible Race.* Berkeley: University of California Press, 1966.

ENGLUND, S. "The University and Its Reform—Sweden." Report No. 11, Conference on University Reforms, Ragaz, 20–21 April 1970, Institute of the European Community for University Studies (stencilled).

FLOUD, J. E., HALSEY, A. H., AND MARTIN, F. M. *Social Class and Educational Opportunity.* London: Heineman, 1956.

FREIRE, P. *Pedagogy of the Oppressed.* New York: Herder & Herder, 1970.

GARMS, W. I. "The Correlates of Educational Effort: A Multivariate Analysis." *Comparative Education Review,* Oct. 1968, *12,* 281–290.

GRIGNON, C., AND PASSERON, J. C. *Innovation in Higher Education: French Experience before 1968.* Paris: OECD, 1970.

HANSEN, W. L., AND WEISBROD, B. A. *Costs and Finance of Public Higher Education.* Chicago: Markham, 1969.

HARBISON, F., AND MYERS, C. A. *Education, Manpower and Economic Growth.* New York: McGraw-Hill, 1964.

HARBISON, F., AND MYERS, C. A. (Eds.) *Manpower and Education; Country Studies in Economic Development.* New York: McGraw-Hill, 1965.

HARBISON, F., MARUHNIC, J., AND RESNICK, J. R. *Quantitative Analyses of Modernization and Development.* Princeton: Industrial Relations Section, Princeton University, 1970.

HAVIGHURST, R. "Education, Social Mobility and Social Change in Four Societies: A Comparative Study." In K. I. Gezi (Ed.), *Education in Comparative and International Perspectives.* New York: Holt-Rinehart & Winston, 1971, pp. 262–279.

ILLICH, I. D. *Deschooling Society.* New York: Harper & Row, 1971.

Institute for Social Research, University of Zagreb. *Innovation in Higher Education: Reforms in Yugoslavia.* Paris: OECD, 1970.

International Committee for University Emergency. *Intercultural Education.* New York, January, 1971.

LILGE, F. *Abuse of Learning: The Failure of the German University.* New York: Macmillan, 1948.

OECD. *Case Studies of Innovation in Higher Education: Common Outline.* Paris, 1967a.

OECD. *Educational Policy and Planning: Netherlands.* Paris, 1967b.

OECD. *Educational Policy and Planning: Sweden.* Paris, 1967c.

OECD. *Educational Policy and Planning: Austria.* Paris, 1968.

OECD. *The Development of Higher Education: Quantitative Trends.* Paris, 1969a.

OECD. *Reviews of National Policies for Education: Ireland*. Paris, 1969b.

OECD. *Reviews of National Policies for Education: Italy*. Paris, 1969c.

OECD. *Reviews of National Policies for Education: Sweden*. Paris, 1969d.

OECD. Conference on Policies for Educational Growth. *Group Disparities in Educational Participation*. Background Study No. 4. Paris, 1970a (STP-70-9), 14–15 (mimeographed).

OECD. Conference on Policies for Educational Growth. *Changes in Secondary and Higher Education*. Background Study No. 6. Paris, 1970b (STP-70-11), (mimeographed).

OECD. *Planning New Structures of Post-Secondary Education; Short-Cycle Higher Education: Trends and Issues*. Paris, 1970c, DAS/EID/70.31.

OECD. *Planning New Structures of Post-Secondary Education: Country Statement; USA*. Paris, 1970d, DAS/EID/70.24.07.

OECD. *Planning New Structures of Post-Secondary Education: Country Statement; Japan*. Paris, 1970e, DAS/EID/70.24.21.

OECD. *Review of National Policies for Education: Austria*. Paris, 1970f.

OECD. *Review of National Policies for Education; Japan, Examiner's Report and Questions*. Paris, 1970g, ED(70) 2.

OECD. *Development of Higher Education: 1950–1967, Analytical Report*. Paris, 1971a.

OECD. *Review of National Policies for Education: France*. Paris, 1971b.

OECD. *Review of National Policies for Education; Germany, Examiner's Report and Questions*. Paris, 1971c, ED(71) 19.

OECD. *Reviews of National Policies for Education: United States*. Paris, 1971d.

OECD. *Towards New Structures of Post-Secondary Education: A Preliminary Statement of Issues*. Paris, 1971e.

PASSIN, H. *Society and Education in Japan*. New York: Teachers College Press, 1965.

PENNAR, J., BAKALO, I., AND BEREDAY, G. Z. F. *Modernization and Diversity in Soviet Education*. New York: Praeger, 1971.

PERKIN, H. J. *Innovation in Higher Education: New Universities in the United Kingdom*. Paris: OECD, 1969.

Report of the Committee on the Age of Majority. London: HMSO, Comd 3347, 1967.

RINGER, F. *The Decline of the German Mandarins: The German Academic Community, 1890–1933*. Cambridge, Mass.: Harvard University Press, 1969.

SNYDERS, K. J. "University Reforms in the Netherlands." Institut de la communaute europeenne pour les etudes universitaires, *l'Universite et sa reforme*. Ragaz Conference, 1970.

INDEX

A

Academic freedom: minimum definition of, 126–128; and public control, 120–138; public pressure on, 122–124; and university survival, 124–128

Admissions, liberalization of, 5–6, 142–143

Australia, higher education in: and community services, 12; continuing education, 132, 133; by television teaching, 78

Austria, higher education in: geographic inequities of, 49; student population and, 33; women students and, 50

B

Belgium, higher education in: curricular reform and, 110; democratization of, 43; racial inequities of, 52; student population and, 33; women students and, 51

Binary system: as democratization process, 44–45; as structural reform, 60–62, 75

C

Canada, higher education in: and continuing education, 132; curricular reform in, 108, 109, 112; enrollment increase in, 20–23; extramural impact of, 128, 130; faculty recruitment and, 92, 94; governance and faculty power in, 94, 96; inequities in, 48, 52, 53; prestige patterns in, 77; public control of, 121; public pressures on, 124; reform in, 4–18, 108, 109, 112; subuniversities in, 59, 64, 73; teaching-research priorities in, 89; unregulated studies in, 118–119; women students and, 51; work-study programs and, 116

Chair system: converted to department system, 7–8, 94–95, 113; in governance and faculty power, 84, 85

China, higher education in: elitism in, 39; work-study programs in, 117

Colombia, higher education in: and continuing education, 132; subuniversity achitecture, 69; and television teaching, 78

154